THE BOSTON TERRIER

An American Original

USA 20c

Beagle, Boston Terrier

*This stamp was one of four issued in 1984 by the United States Post Office.
It was designed by Roy Anderson in celebration of the 100th anniversary of
the American Kennel Club.*

THE BOSTON TERRIER

An American Original

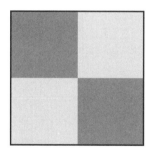

Beverly and Michael Staley

**HOWELL
BOOK
HOUSE**

Macmillan • USA

Howell Book House
A Prentice Hall Macmillan Company
15 Columbus Circle
New York, NY 10023

MACMILLAN is a registered trademark of Macmillan, Inc.
Library of Congress Cataloging-in-Publication Data

ISBN: 0-87605-056-9

Manufactured in the United States of America
10 9 8 7 6 5 4 3 2 1

DEDICATION

This book is dedicated to our daughter, Jennifer, and our son, Jeffrey, who grew up with the dogs, attending dog shows on weekends, helping raise and train puppies, and showing dogs themselves.

The authors' Ch. Staley's El–Bo's Showman, a multiple Best in Show winner and sire of fifty–four champions.

Contents

An American Original—drawing of a Boston Terrier by Ann Baker, Florida.

Acknowledgments

We wish to thank first those who directly helped us with the development of this book:

Kathryn T. Graves, PhD., of Georgetown, Kentucky, who wrote the chapter on Genetics and who is currently conducting research at the University of Kentucky to develop a blood test that identifies carriers of juvenile cateracts.

Alicia Parry of Syracuse, New York, who wrote the chapter on Obedience and who is actively involved with Obedience training with her Bostons and has also served as Obedience Chairman for the Boston Terrier Club of America.

Peggy D. Jackson and Vickie Kwasny, for the line drawings of Boston Terriers, and Lisa Braunstein–La Mere, for photos illustrating the Standard.

All of the many breeders and exhibitors who donated photographs used in this book.

Next we wish to thank all those people who have taught us so much over the years about the showing and breeding of Boston Terriers, who have shared their knowledge of the breed and who have taught us about the breeding of Boston Terriers, and who have anticipated each new litter with us.

We would also like to give special acknowledgment to Jim and Mina Lehn, John LoPorto, Marie Ferguson, Ray Perso, Mary Ann Caruso, Bud and Celeste Schulte, Juanita Camp, Bob Candland, and Leonard Myers—all of whom have given us invaluable insight into the breeding and exhibiting of Boston Terriers.

Introduction

Boston Terriers are many things to different people. To the pet owner they are a part of the family. A Boston is a watchdog and companion to the elderly who live alone and a playmate and clown to the young child. They are trained as therapy dogs to visit nursing homes. Bostons are perhaps the most beautiful of all show dogs to the conformation exhibitor and the smartest of all dogs to the Obedience exhibitor. To the breeder, Bostons are that picture of perfection that we hope to breed someday, perhaps only a generation or two from now.

Above all else, however, the Boston Terrier is a loving, affectionate companion who never questions Why but only What. Grace, style, beauty, and intelligence make this breed the perfect choice for whatever your needs are. Bostons ask so little from you in return for unwaivering devotion.

Now that the first century of the Boston Terrier has passed, it is with the greatest enthusiasm that we look forward to what lies ahead in the future of our breed. In the first century this little dog brought happiness and delight to many thousands of households throughout the length and breadth of this land and around the world.

Who could ever have realized this American Original would eventually be created from those early breedings? But then, maybe those forefathers of the breed really knew what they were doing as they bred and occasionally brought in new blood just as it was needed to refine the breed. Perhaps they too had a vision of what that perfect Boston Terrier was to be in both conformation and spirit. Perhaps the vision they held and worked to achieve was not too different from ours. Perhaps if we go back and look at the original Standard we will see just what changes have occurred in the last hundred years and how the vision of the Boston Terrier, an American Original, has gradually changed in the second century. Revisions of the original Standard have changed weight classifications, preferences in color, and bite, but mainly they have added more detail to clarify the Standard. The old Standard did not allot any points for general appearance and expression, which are so important to the Boston Terrier. Neither the old Standard nor our present Standard allots any points to temperament, the one quality that most defines the breed.

Only time will tell how the Standard will be revised in the next hundred years, but since the Boston Terrier Club of America has so many dedicated breeders we are confident that the Standard will be intact at the end of the second hundred years—with the possible exception of a need to ban cropped ears and simply breed Boston Terriers with better ears.

THE BOSTON TERRIER

An American Original

Fascination, whelped in 1906.

Ch. Ravenroyd Rockefeller, whelped in 1925.

CHAPTER

┌───┐
│ 1 │
└───┘

Origin and Beginnings of the Boston Terrier Breed

OVER A CENTURY HAS PASSED SINCE THAT EVENTFUL BREEDING THAT WAS TO create the first American-bred Boston Terrier, the breed destined to be one of the finest of all companion dogs.

In 1865 Robert C. Hooper of Boston imported Hooper's Judge from England. Judge was a cross between an English Bulldog and a White English Terrier. Judge was then bred to an English Bulldog bitch, Burnett's Gyp, owned by Edward Burnett of Massachusetts. Hooper's Judge was a 32-pound dog, high-on-leg, dark brindle with white face markings. Burnett's Gyp was a white Bulldog, short faced, stockily built, and short stationed with a three-quarter tail. This breeding produced Wells' Eph, a short-stationed, evenly marked, dark brindle. Wells' Eph was then bred to Tobin's Kate, a smaller, short-headed, golden brindle dog, which produced Bernard's Tom, whelped in 1877.

By 1891, the early breeders, who had kept records of all their breedings, had applied to the American Kennel Club to register their distinct breed of dogs, known as Round Heads. On March 31, 1891, Charles

Patsy Ringmaster.

Bernard's Tom, the most important founder of the breed.

Leland held the first meeting of breeders. The first Standard for the breed was presented a week later, on April 7.

To correct uneven type in the early breedings, a bully-type bitch would be bred to a Bull Terrier and a too-terrier-type bitch would be bred to a Bulldog. French Bulldogs were also occasionally used to help establish type and to reduce size in these early breedings. In 1891, the breeders established a Stud Register showing about seventy-five dogs whose ancestors could be traced for three complete generations. These dogs proved to be the foundation stock of today's Boston Terriers.

Bernard's Tom was bred to Kelly's Nell, a dark brindle of even markings, weighing approximately twenty pounds. From this breeding came Bernard's Mike, who had the large, full, round eyes that became so important to the breed. He was a light brindle color with white markings and weighed approximately twenty-five pounds. Mike also had another quality favored by early breeders—a short crew tail. He sired the first Boston to be registered by the American Kennel Club, who was named Punch.

These dogs were first exhibited in the New England Kennel Club show in Boston in April 1888, at which time they were shown in classes for Round-Headed Bull Terriers. These dogs were originally called American Bull Terriers, but upon being admitted to the American Kennel Club Stud Book in 1893 the name was changed to Boston Terrier.

In the years before 1900, only four Boston Terriers completed their championships: Topsy, Spider, Monte, and Tansy. Monte was sired by Goode's Buster, a rich mahogany brindle with even face markings. Buster and Monte sired close to 20 percent of the registered Boston Terriers prior to 1900.

ESTABLISHING TYPE

We consider it a real stroke of brilliance that the early breeders used the Bulldog as the mother of the Boston Terrier and the Bull Terrier, a cross between the English Bulldog and the White English Terrier, as the father. These two breeds contained enough of the Bulldog heredity to stabilize the resulting breed.

The establishment of type was the most difficult task for the early breeders. It was the French Bulldog that was of great help in establishing

Ch. Million Dollar King, whelped in 1920.

the desired type. Since the French Bulldog was the result of inbreeding some English Bulldogs belonging to the lace makers of Nottingham, this genealogy made French Bulldogs the perfect choice to assist in the improvement of the Boston Terrier breed. Occasionally you will still see a Boston Terrier that is a throwback to the French Bulldog crosses that were done by the early breeders.

It is amazing that out of all these early breedings, varying so greatly in size and color, the forefathers of our breed were able to produce as much uniformity as quickly as they did. That is not to say that these dogs were anywhere near the quality of today's Boston Terriers. They had much improvement ahead in establishing type in body, head, color, markings, and size.

Although the original weighed approximately thirty pounds, there was immediately a decided variation in weight, with much popularity being accorded to the smaller Boston—so much popularity, in fact, that there was a Toy class for Boston Terriers under twelve pounds. Eventually this class was eliminated and the divisions were changed to under fifteen pounds, fifteen to twenty pounds, and twenty to twenty-five pounds.

Even greater than the variation in size was that in color and markings. Behind the Boston Terrier were the white specimens of the English Bulldog, the dark brindle Bull Terrier, the mismarks, and the splash markings. With all these variations of colors and markings, it is amazing that the Boston Terrier breeds as true as it does.

Ch. Judd's Miss Libby, owned by Mrs. Harry Judd of Kentucky.

CHAPTER

2

Development of Early Lines

AMONG THE MOST IMPORTANT SIRES IN THE EARLY YEARS WAS **SULLIVAN'S PUNCH**, a *white* Boston Terrier with irregular brindle face markings, who was owned by C. F. Sullivan of Massachusetts. His most notable offspring were Lord Derby and Lady Dainty.

Goode's Buster, owned by Alex Goode of Boston, produced a number of remarkable Boston Terriers, which all exceeded him in quality. The best of his get was Monte. Monte not only was one of the greatest show winners of his day, but he also produced many other show winners and producers of quality Boston Terriers.

Bixby's Tony Boy produced dogs of smaller size and brought a rich dark color to his get. Cracksman, a grandson of Goode's Buster, brought expression and a tendency toward a lighter-colored coat to the breed.

From the strain of Sullivan's Punch and Goode's Buster, Derby Boy II was produced. He was a small dog, short in station, *without* required face markings, and bully in type. He produced offspring with short backs and well-ribbed bodies with good heads and conformation. Derby Boy produced Ch. Derby Boy's Gift, but another Derby Boy son, Bunkio Derby, was a much more important producer. He excelled in head and was a clean, big dog.

Ch. Long's Brat's Witch, winner of fifteen Best in Show Awards.

Sport IV (Ringmaster), whelped in 1902.

Hagerty's King, whelped in 1916.

Mosholu Blink, whelped in 1917.

The **Ringmaster** strain was remarkable for its producing ability. The strain began with Sport IV. He himself was overdone, but he produced Boston Terriers that excelled in expression. Sport produced Ch. Todd Boy, who was a beautiful show dog. Todd Boy had a brother, Ringleader, who produced Ch. Dallen's Sport and Ch. Lady Ringleader. Another son, Billy Ringmaster, produced Tony Ringmaster and Bessie Ringmaster. Bessie's daughter, Patsy Ringmaster, was a small dog who carried on her strain's remarkable producing ability to her son Invader, which he in turn passed on to his son Tiny Ringmaster.

The **Raffles** strain was founded on a trim little terrier dog, Heilborn's Raffles. He sired Ch. Dallen's Spider, Ch. Trimount, and Ch. Major Raffles. Spider sired Ch. Peter's King, who was a great producer and finished his championship in spite of having a half-white head. Mosholu Blink and Woodward Captain were descendants of the Raffles strain and both were equally good producers.

EARLY BREEDERS AND THEIR DOGS

By the 1920s, this new upstart breed had achieved popularity far beyond the wildest dreams of the early breeders. *From 1920 to 1963 the Boston Terrier was the only breed to claim the distinction of being ranked continuously in the top ten* of American Kennel Club registrations.

We can look back now to the pedigrees of the early years and see that in the early 1900s Goode's Buster, Tony Boy, Sullivan's Punch, and Cracksman were prominent in three strains—the Derby strain founded by Derby Boy II, the Ringmaster strain founded by Sport IV, and the Raffles strain founded by Heilborn Raffles. By the 1920s, these three strains had produced the following six pillars of the breed: Champion Hagerty's King, Ch. Mosholu Blink, Sigourney King, Woodward Captain, Intruder, and Ch. Prince Conde. The first of these, Champion Hagerty's King, was said to be one of the most perfect Boston Terriers ever bred. He was a 14-pound dog with a faultless head and muzzle representing the perfect type, being neither too terrier nor too bully.

The early breeders were located primarily in Massachusetts and New York, but as the breed developed and the popularity of the Boston Terrier increased prominent owners and breeders were beginning to show up in the Midwest and the West. In the West, Mrs. W. E. Porter founded

Ch. Rockefeller's Ace

Ch. Kramer's Little Chappie

Ch. H M S Kiddie Boots Son

the **Kingway** Kennels (later to be Leonard Myers' Kennel name) in the Rocky Mountains. Despite being in a remote area with few shows, she managed to finish seventeen champions.

Alva Rosenberg of New York, the highly acclaimed all-breed judge, won Winners Dog at Westminster in 1926 with his Ch. Ravenroyd Rockefeller, later owned by E.H. Morse of Flint, Michigan. Rockefeller, a 25-pound Boston with good balance and refinement, was the sire of seven champions including Int. Ch. Rockefeller's Ace, winner of Best in Breed at Morris and Essex in 1934 and owned by W. C. Ely of Zionsville, Pennsylvania.

In New York, the **Hagerty** Kennel owned by A. Droll and Benny Rosenbloom at one time promoted eleven stud dogs. The most famous of these was Ch. Hagerty Again, who sired sixteen champions including Ch. Royal Kid. Even in the 1990s, a black spot in the white blaze on the top of the Boston Terrier's skull is still referred to as a Hagerty mark by many old-time breeders, as this was a frequent characteristic of the Hagerty line.

In Chicago, Dr. Gustav Brandle whelped the famous duo Ch. Rockabye Tunney and Ch. Rockabye Dempsey on the night of the famous Dempsey–Tunney fight in Chicago. Ch. Rockabye Dempsey, owned by Hilda Ridder of New York City, was a 14-pound Boston of mahogany color and was one of the more popular sires of his day. Mrs. Ridder also was the owner of Ch. O'Glo's Midgie, who won two Best in Show awards.

Sarah Dowser of Detroit owned Ch. Detroit Million Dollar Girl, who was the first Boston Terrier bitch to go Best in Show. Myrtle Hayhurst of Bourbonnais, Illinois, owned the great sire Int. Ch. Flash Again, who produced eleven champions who in turn established the **Flash Again** line. He was a 15-pound dog whose pedigree went back to Ringmaster and Ch. Hagerty's King.

Mrs. E. P. Anders of Allentown, Pennsylvania, owned the **Royal** Kennels, which was the home of Royal Kid. Royal Kid sired twenty-three champions, the most famous of whom was Ch. Royal Kid Regards, who won four Best in Show awards and sired eighteen champions. The Royal Kid strain were small Bostons with good heads, eyes, and markings.

Mrs. Claude Fitzgerald of Wyandotte, Michigan, owned Ch. **Regardless**, who sired thirty-three champions. The most famous of these was Ch.

15

Ch. Gentleman Jim Regardless II, owned by Mr. and Mrs. Claude Fitzgerald.

Ch. Chappie's Little Man, owned by Charles D. Cline, winner of seven Best in Show Awards.

Ch. Mighty Sweet Regardless II, owned by Mr. and Mrs. Claude Fitzgerald

Mighty Sweet Regardless, who won twenty-one Best in Shows. She also placed first in the Group at Westminster in both 1947 and 1948.

Ch. Griffings Little Chappie, who was bred by Mr. and Mrs. Robert Griffing, was sold to Signe Carlson of Englewood, California, where he sired nineteen champions.

All of these show that even in the early days good Boston Terriers received recognition—even in the stiffest competition.

Ch. Globe Glowing Perfection, owned by Vincent Perry.

Ch.B.B.'s Kim of Fellow, bred by Billie Niegenfeld and owned by Bud and Celeste Schulte.

CHAPTER

3

The Breed Advances

Later Top Winners and Top Producers

THERE IS NOT ENOUGH TIME OR SPACE TO LIST ALL OF THE BREED'S TOP producers in the last few decades, but we would like to mention some of the great ones briefly.

Vincent Perry's Ch. Globe Glowing Perfection, who, in addition to compiling a nice show record, produced fifteen champions. Ch. Globe Glowing All By Himself produced eighteen champions. Although Perfection was a Best in Show winner, Mr. Perry considered Ch. Globe Glowing All By Himself the better sire of the two. The **Globe Glowing** line of Mr. Perry's can be found at the back of today's top lines. Vincent Perry was "Mr. Boston Terrier" and, in addition to being a well-known actor, will always be remembered as the foremost author, judge, and breeder of Boston Terriers.

Ch. B-B's Kim of Fellow, owned by Celeste C. Schulte of Ohio, was a Best in Show winner and the sire of ten champions, including Best in Show winner Ch. Taffy's Kid Benjamin. Both Celeste and her husband, Raphael Schulte, the all-breed judge, had a good eye for Bostons and did

Ch. Iowana's Fancy boots, owned by Florence Dancer.

Ch. Taffy's Kid Benjamin, winner of ten Best in Show Awards.

Ch.Grant's Royal Command, Best in Show winner and sire of thirty-six champions, owned by Louise Grant.

Ch. Royalty Iowana Jetaway, owned by Marie Ferguson.

Ch. Top's Again's Duke of Regards, owned by James Trelease and handled by Marie Ferguson.

much to promote the breed. Their **Sunnyhaven** Kennels produced many lovely Boston Terriers.

Florence Dancer bred two Best in Show winners, Ch. Iowana's Velvet Coquette and Ch. Iowana's Fancy Flair. She also bred Iowana's Fancy Boots Model, who was the sire of eleven champions. The **Iowana** line is another great line of Boston Terriers that are still behind many of today's pedigrees.

Louise Grant not only had a Best in Show winner in Ch. Royale Command's Ebony Prince, but she also produced yet another Best in Show winner in Ch. Grant's Royal Command. He sired thirty-six champions, and Ch. Grant's Royale Command II sired twenty-four champions. Ch. Grant's Royal Command is another dog who has greatly influenced the breed and is still to be found behind many of our present-day dogs. Both Florence Dancer and Louise Grant were well-respected judges of the breed.

Leonard Myers of **Kingway** Bostons in Colorado has been breeding Bostons since 1935. His stock is from the Iowana, Command, and Unique lines. Mr. Myers has been an AKC-approved judge of Boston Terriers for over thirty years and has judged the Boston Terrier Club of America show several times, most recently he judged the 100th Anniversary Show in Boston, in 1991.

In the East, Dr. K. Eileen Hite, who at one time was the editor of the *Boston Bulletin*, was the owner of Ch. Chappie's Little Stardust. He sired twenty-one champions, two of whom were Ch. Star Q's Brass Button and Ch. Star Q's Pease Knutu.

Multiple Best in Show winner Ch. Good Time Charlie T. Brown, owned by Tom Enwright of Florida, sired eighteen champions. Ch. DeMent's Handsome Crusader, owned by J. T. DeMent of Missouri, sired twenty-two champions.

Jill Ritchey of Ohio not only had a Best in Show winner in Ch. Milady Deacon of Boston, but she also had a top-producing stud dog in Ch. Alexander Star Reward.

In Missouri, Ch. Royal Show Man, owned by Pearl Ruble and Shirley Canale, produced thirteen champions; Russell Dowell kept that line going strong with his top-producing Ch. Finales Good News.

Marie Ferguson of Chicago did much to improve the breed with her Ch. Tops Again's Duke of Regards, who produced twenty-one

Ch. Toy Town's High Stepping Tammy, Best in Show winner and owned by John LoPorto of Chicago.

Ch. Royalty's Special Beau, owned by Mr. and Mrs. W. C. Richardson.

Ch. Zodiac's Special Beau, a multiple Best in Show winner and one of the all-time producing sires in the breed, bred by Juanita Camp and owned by Bob Breum.

Ch. Rowdy Dowdy of Romance, a multiple Best in Show winner bred by Rose Coulter of Oklahoma and owned by Charles H. Schmidt of Indiana.

Ch. Kimkev's Benchmark, owned by Susan and Ed Adams of Georgia.

champions including Ch. Toy Town's Hi Stepping Star Trek; he in turn sired thirteen champions. Marie was an excellent handler, and every Boston she ever had was beautifully groomed. Among the many clients' dogs she showed was John LoPorto's Ch. Toy Town High Stepping Tammy, who was not only a Best in Show winner but also the dam of six champions.

In Washington, Cora Brat's Ch. Long Brat Witch IV was a beautiful Boston Terrier bitch who won a Best in Show. Another Best in Show winner was Harry Judd's Ch. Judd's Miss Libby in Kentucky.

In Iowa, Eva and Irwin Krueger's Ch. Beau Kay's Dusty Tops Again produced eleven champions, one of whom was Ch. Unique's Special Beau (sire of Ch. Zodiac's Special Beau), and their Ch. Unique's Royalty Kid produced ten champions, including Juanita Camp's Ch. Unique's Star of Zodiac. The latter was the dam of Bob Breum's Best in Show winner Ch. Zodiac's Special Beau, who sired forty-six champions and was one of best-showing and -producing Boston Terriers of all time. Juanita Camp is presently publishing a Boston Terrier newsletter for the breed, along with being involved in various animal rights groups.

Ch. Unique's Special Beau also had a grandson, Ch. Sabe's Unique Choice, who sired nine champions and was owned by Sharon Saberton.

Julius and Willie Martell of Kansas produced quite a few champions in a short period of time by breeding good-quality stock to Bob Breum's Ch. Zodiac's Special Beau. Among the most famous were Ch. Maestro's Billy Whiz Bang, who was a Best in Show winner owned by Bob Breum, and Ch. Maestro's Sophie's Choice, owned by Mary Alice and Joseph Niebauer of Michigan.

Art and Lil Huddleston of California began their line of **Showbiz** Bostons from the Regards and Regardless bloodlines. Art began to collect Boston Terrier memorabilia from all over the country and soon had the nation's largest collection. Art made a contribution to the breed by writing a monthly column in the *Boston Bulletin* for many years. He also contributed articles for the breed column in the *Gazette*. In addition, he wrote the book *The Boston Terrier*, which was published in 1985.

Andy Turner's Ch. Dusty Tops Again Special produced fifteen champions, and his Ch. Tops Again Gay Pepper produced fourteen.

Ch. Karadin Jim Dandy, owned by Mary Lou Zimmerman of Pennsylvania.

Ch. Fascinating Fancy Chief, owned by Joseph and Mary Alice Niebauer.

Ch. Bo-K's Rambo, bred by Bob and Karen Milham and owned by Betty C. Wells of Tennessee.

Ch. Zodiac's Special Warrior, owned by Earl and Mildred Gentry of Florida.

Ch. Yoki-En's Couragous Challenge, bred and owned by Alice and Mary Ochiai of California.

Ch. Steele's Ancoram Top Gun, bred by Marilyn and Norman Randall and owned by Hazel Steele of Maryland.

Tom and Sue Ghaster of Ohio produced quite a few champions from their Ch. Tops Again Brandy, Ch. Top Shelf Sweet Lou, and Ch. Top Shelf Little Travelin Man.

Ch. M. L.'s Ace High, owned by Mary Lou Zimmerman Dreher of Pennsylvania, sired seventeen champions.

Ch. Court Barton Emerald Isle sired eleven champions, among whom were Ethel Braunstein's Ch. Karadin Kiss Me Kate and Ch. Karadin Our Mariah. Today, Ethel is one of the most knowledgeable breeders, authors, and judges of Boston Terriers. She was also instrumental in the revision of the Boston Terrier Standard of February 1990.

Ch. Bo-K's Nu Masterpiece of Model, owned by Bob and Karen Milham of Arizona, sired eleven champions.

Ch. El-Bo's Rudy is a Dandy, owned by Bob and Eleanor Candland of California, was as good a Boston Terrier as one could want to see. He was a multiple Best in Show winner, having won eighteen all-breed Bests in Show; and he sired fifty-eight champions. Among his get is Ch. Staley's El-Bo's Showman, who is also a multiple Best in Show winner and the sire of fifty-six champions, among whom is Ch. Justamere's Showman's De Ja Vu. De Ja Vu is the sire of twenty-five champions including the Best in Show winner Ch. O.J. First Class Fortune Cooky. Both De Ja Vu and Fortune Cooky were owned by Joanne Hearst. "Cooky," as she was known, and Ch. Justamere's C'est Simone were both tragically lost in June 1993 when they were poisoned by a neighbor's pesticides.

There is a long list of breeders who have not been discussed here, such as Gil Dishongh, Leone Brown Kelly, Ray Perso, and Warren Ubberoth, who not only affected the breed but were respected judges of the Boston Terrier. These breeders have worked hard to improve the quality of their breeding and have spent much of their time helping novice breeders to establish quality breeding practices. It is to these dedicated breeders that the future of the Boston Terrier belongs. It is only through cooperation and friendly competition that the quality of Boston Terriers can gradually improve in future generations.

Our breed Standard has painted the picture of the perfect Boston Terrier in our minds and hearts, and eventually it will be bred, possibly by you.

Ch. El-Bo's Wind Chime Pattie, bred and owned by Bob and
Eleanor Candland of California.

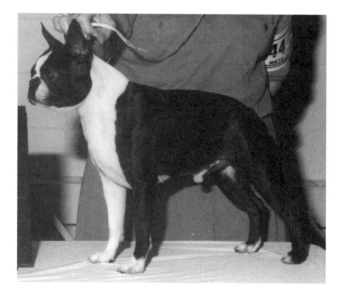

Ch. Kap's Beau by Sunny, a Best in Show winner, owned by
Connie Page of Missouri.

THE PARENT CLUB

The Boston Terrier Club of America, from its original organization in 1891, has been centered in and around Boston, Massachusetts. This club underwent complete reorganization during the early 1980s and has since emerged as a truly national club represented by officers from every region of the country. These changes were brought about by the work of many dedicated members, including Helen Duncan, Kathleen Kelly, Mina Lehn, and Mira Jilbert.

In 1985 the Boston Terrier Club of America held its first floating Specialty show in Ft. Mitchell, Kentucky; each year the show moves to a different location. In 1991 the Boston Terrier Club of America returned the National Specialty to Hyannis, Massachusetts, for the Centennial Celebration, where there were 268 Boston Terriers for a total of 482 entries.

An American Original.

CHAPTER

4

Choosing the Right Puppy

What to Look For

NOW THAT YOU HAVE DECIDED THAT THIS IS THE RIGHT BREED FOR YOU, YOU are about to embark upon the task of finding the right Boston Terrier. At this point we must differentiate between buying a Boston Terrier puppy for a pet and buying one for show and/or breeding.

THE FAMILY PET

If your search is for a Boston Terrier to meet your family's needs for a pet, you can begin by obtaining the name of the secretary of your local Boston Terrier Club from the American Kennel Club. If you have no local club in your area, you can contact the secretary of the Boston Terrier Club of America to put you in touch with the Breeder Referral Chairperson, who will supply you with a list of reputable breeders in your area.

Before you begin viewing prospective litters, you need to decide whether a male or a female puppy best suits you and your family. With a bitch puppy, you will be facing two heats a year unless she is spayed.

Boston Terrier puppies, owned by Frank Guemple.

A male puppy, on the other hand, takes a little extra training to keep him from "lifting" his leg to "mark" his territory. We have heard some people comment that females make more affectionate pets, but some of our most affectionate Boston Terriers have been males. So this is primarily a matter of personal preference. The main thing that you will want to do is to find the healthiest, best-looking specimen that you can afford. If you have friends who are knowledgeable about Boston Terriers, they should accompany you on your search for a Boston puppy.

As you inspect each litter, always ask to see the mother and at least a photo of the father. If the parents are not what you are looking for, you can be assured that the puppies will not be either, as they probably will inherit the parents' physical characteristics and many of their personality traits. Remember, all Boston Terriers are cute as puppies, but they do not all necessarily turn out that way.

You will want your puppy to be healthy, active, alert, and very curious. Watch the puppies as they eat and play to observe their individual personalities. Check the puppies for deafness by making a noise when the puppy isn't looking and checking the response. The puppy should be neither overweight nor underweight. A fat belly can be a sign of worms, and a thin puppy can be a sign of sickness or undernourishment. Check the puppy for signs of overall good health. Select the puppy with "spirit," and avoid the puppy that is unusually shy or timid. Check movement to make sure that the puppy is not lame. Look over the puppy's surroundings. Cleanliness is often a good indication of the care that has been given to the litter. Check the puppy's temperature, and check for loose stools if possible. The puppy's skin should be clean and free of fleas, ringworm, and mange. The coat should be clean and be a color accepted in the Standard. The breeder should explain what type of diet the puppy is on and also what inoculations and medical treatment the puppy has had thus far.

If you are primarily interested in a Boston Terrier as a family pet, the Boston Terrier you choose need not be the perfect embodiment of the standard. As long as the pup fulfills the requirements of the Standard in temperament and general appearance, he or she need not follow the Standard to the letter to bring the joy of owning a Boston Terrier to you and your family. Many Boston Terrier owners have considered their dog, who is the center of attention in their family, to be far superior to some of the top-ranked Boston Terrier show dogs in the country. Many pet owners never really look beyond a puppy's personality and cuteness, and that is fine as long as you do not change your mind and later decide that you want a puppy for show purposes.

THE SHOW PROSPECT

If, on the other hand, you are looking for a Boston Terrier puppy to show and to breed, then in addition to noting all of the health, temperament, and personality attributes, you need to make sure that the puppy you choose closely follows the Standard and has quality Boston Terriers in its pedigree.

The easiest way to be sure that your puppy is close to the Standard is to look for a puppy who is mature enough to see how it will develop. So many puppies who seem full of promise at six weeks of age do not fulfill their owners' expectations by the time they are one year old. Many a prospective exhibitor has been deeply disappointed by a fantastic puppy who developed into a mediocre adult dog.

A Family Tree

The puppy's pedigree can be one of the most important criteria in choosing a Boston Terrier. If you have familiarized yourself with the puppies' ancestors by studying the breed, you will know if they possess the qualities you are looking for. If the puppies' ancestors were all good, typey Bostons, then the chances of the puppies turning out well are indeed good. If, on the other hand, the puppies' pedigrees are composed primarily of pet Boston Terriers of unknown quality, you have a vastly diminished chance of these puppies turning out to be outstanding representatives of the breed.

Suppose that a potential puppy possessed a pedigree of above-average ancestors on both sides, it is time to stop and evaluate on the pup's own merits. Begin the evaluation with general appearance. Stand back and check the puppy's overall balance and structure, the front, rear, and topline. Remember, though, that puppies change in structure as they grow. It is possible to see the squareness of the head and the shortness and depth of the muzzle. Remember that although a good flat muzzle is what you are looking for, the muzzle must also have depth. The puppy should also have large, round, dark eyes with a "God love it" look. The pup's head should be cleancut and free from wrinkles, and it should possess the required head markings and good ear set with small erect ears that hopefully will not need to be cropped.

Although the Standard calls for even *or* undershot bite, you will find that a slightly undershot puppy possesses a squarer underjaw.

Look for good bone substance in the puppy's legs and a nice straight front. The puppy should have a good strong rear with good angulation and nice short hocks. If the puppy's tail seems a bit long, do not worry as the dog will grow into it. Look for a level topline that rolls off at the rump. Check the puppy for correct gait. Remember that a puppy goes through different stages of development and can "fall apart" on you during adolescence, although not all puppies do. Those puppies that "fall apart" can and usually do come together again as they mature, but there is no guarantee that this will happen.

Once again, if the parents and grandparents on both sides of the pedigree are all sound Bostons of correct type, the odds that the puppy will be a sound Boston of correct type are greatly increased. If the breeder from whom you are purchasing this puppy consistently produces sound typey puppies, once again your odds are greatly increased. If you are dealing with a breeder who maintains quality breeding stock and who consistently breeds to top quality stud dogs, the price of the puppies may be higher than those of a breeder who breeds whoever happens to be in season to the most convenient and reasonable stud dog.

Remember that no matter how perfect a puppy seems to be at eight weeks of age, there is a vast array of problems that can crop up in the first year. Many an owner of a beautiful Boston Terrier puppy has been greatly upset to find that the perfect puppy purchased now has too much white in the eyes, a tongue that shows, a poor front, or a weak rear.

The only thing that you can be sure of in an eight-week-old puppy is color and markings. And you must keep in mind that the black markings will slightly overtake the white as the puppy matures. Even size can sometimes turn out to be a problem, for a puppy may never quite grow enough even to qualify for the under-fifteen-pound class, or the puppy may eventually exceed the twenty-five-pound weight limit. You should consider

Ch. Alexander's Thunder, bred and owned by Dr. Jim and Linda Alexander of Georgia.

yourself extremely fortunate if your puppy holds true to earlier promise and turns out to be everything that you hoped, for no breeder can or should promise you that your eight-week-old puppy will definitely be show quality at one year of age. A breeder can only guarantee that the *potential* to be a show quality Boston Terrier is there; you can only hope that it materializes.

Another important fact to remember as you search for your show puppy is that most Boston Terrier breeders are themselves looking for exceptional puppies to show themselves and to breed. For this reason the breeder may have kept the best puppy in the litter, the best may not necessarily be for sale. Acquiring an excellent quality bitch for breeding may also be quite a task. Once you have acquired a really good bitch, you must next find the best possible stud dog to breed her to. You are better off if *you don't own* a stud dog, as you can then search for the stud dog who best complements your bitch. This method of breeding your own show dog is *the most challenging and time consuming,* but there is no greater reward than when you breed that special puppy yourself.

C H A P T E R
5

Care and Training
of Your Puppy

TRAINING IS A TERM THAT COVERS EVERYTHING FROM PAPER TRAINING YOUR
Boston puppy to conformation and obedience training. In this chapter
we will attempt to touch on some of the basic aspects of training.

First we will discuss some of the basic training that every Boston
Terrier puppy requires to adapt to life in your home. We can remember
times when one of our Boston puppies chewed the legs on the dining room
table and another puppy pulled up the tomato plants in the back yard. In
order to enjoy your Boston puppy fully you will need to train the dog to
respect you and your property as well as others and their property. A
Boston puppy old enough to be taken home is old enough to be trained;
you definitely should not expect perfection at this early age, however.

HOUSE MANNERS

One of the first things you will want to do is to paper train your Boston
puppy. Select a spot on the floor near the pup's sleeping area or bed where

a layer of newspaper will be available at all times. When you notice that the puppy is looking for a place to relieve itself, put the puppy on the paper immediately. Praise when your pup is finished. Puppies generally have a bowel movement after eating and urinate after drinking and should be watched closely at these times. Another time to place them on the paper is immediately after awakening. The more frequently you are able to put the puppy on the paper, the sooner your Boston will begin using the paper without your help. When your puppy forgets to use the paper, scold *immediately*. Puppies have short memories and will not know why you are scolding, if you do not scold them when caught in the act. Puppies are quick to pick up the difference in your tone of voice when you are pleased with them and when you are angry. They are eager to please and to win your praise.

By the time you know the schedule and when your pup is ready to go out, housebreaking can begin. Often a puppy will be encouraged if taken to a spot frequented by other dogs. Make sure that you stay out long enough for the pup to relieve itself. If yours does not, try again a little later. When you are successful outside, be sure to give plenty of praise. Try to follow the same schedule that was established for using the paper. After becoming dependable outside, remove the papers and use the outside regularly. It helps to go back to some of the same spots. If an "accident" should occur in the house, scold so that the pup understands this was bad. After becoming housebroken, your puppy will develop a way of letting you know when a trip outside is needed.

THE BASICS

It is very important that every Boston puppy know its name. This can best be accomplished if the owner picks a call name for the puppy and then uses it exclusively. Do not confuse your dog by using other names such as "Pup," "Doggy," and so forth. Once a name has been established the pup should be taught to come on command. This is done by the simple command, "Beans, Come!" Praise for a response to this command ensures that your puppy will always come to you enthusiastically.

You will want to start medical care as soon as you have brought your Boston home. Have your veterinarian give a complete examination to see that the puppy is in good physical condition with no obvious health

Ch. El–Bo's Solo Jellybean, bred and owned by Bob and Eleanor Candland of California.

problems. At this time you will also want to take a fresh stool sample with you to the veterinarian to be sure that the puppy is not infested with any parasites that could keep the puppy from developing to fullest potential. If parasites are present, your veterinarian will prescribe medication to rid your puppy of the worms; you can follow up by having a fresh stool sample checked again in three weeks.

At this time you will also want to check with your veterinarian on continuing your new puppy on a program of basic innoculations begun by the breeder. You might also want to ask about beginning your puppy on a heartworm preventative program.

Your new Boston Terrier will need some special attention at first, but he or she also needs some time alone in a box or crate that can be like the pup's own room in which to sleep. Young puppies need plenty of rest and should be afforded an opportunity to nap after every meal. Puppies may miss their mother or littermates that first night. You may find that it will soothe your puppy if you wrap either a hot water bottle or milk jug full of warm water in a thick towel to snuggle up to during the night. Some people have also found that Boston Terrier puppies are soothed by the ticking of a clock wrapped in a blanket placed in bed with them.

Be sure that everyone in the household knows how to hold the puppy and support its rump and abdomen properly. If small children will be holding the puppy, they should do so only under your supervision and they should hold the puppy only while they are seated. They need to know that *the puppy is not a toy* and needs rest and respect.

CONDITION—HEALTH AND MAINTENANCE

To get your Boston Terrier in good condition, be sure that your dog is neither too fat nor too thin. We have always felt that it is much easier to take weight off some Boston Terriers than it is to put weight on. That may well be because we all can have a tendency to overfeed. In any case, the overweight dog can be brought to the correct weight by gradually decreasing the food consumption and by exercising the dog regularly. This is not only important to the Boston, but is also a real health benefit for the owner.

Ch. Two Shoes One and Only, owned by Dr. Randy Weckman of Kentucky.

We have occasionally found that we have had some picky eaters who do not gain weight easily. These dogs seem to put themselves on a diet and refuse to eat more than they want. For these dogs, we have found a mixture of high calorie ingredients, added to their regular ration, has helped us to achieve a weight gain for dogs who are too thin. These dogs also require regular exercise so that this weight gain is not in the form of excess fat, but will develop into muscle. Following is a recipe for a high caloric supplement that may aid in weight gain for a litter of puppies. *We do not recommend using this mixture on a long-term basis* as it is high in both fat and cholesterol and would not be healthy for your dog to consume throughout a lifetime.

RECIPE FOR QUICK WEIGHT GAIN
    5 pounds ground beef
    2 large boxes Special K (crushed)
    2 boxes Quick Quaker Oats
    2 jars Wheat Germ
    1 dozen eggs
    1 bottle Karo light syrup
    1 cup honey
    1 jar peanut butter (optional)

Mix all of the ingredients together. This will be a somewhat stiff mixture and will take a little time to mix. After the ingredients are well mixed, form into bite-size balls and freeze in individual freezer bags containing enough balls for each feeding for your puppy. When ready to feed, defrost in microwave.

Most Boston Terriers really love this combination and will quickly consume all of the additional calories. We have fed this mixture to puppies until they have attained the additional weight we desired. At that time the Boston can be maintained on regular dog food alone. We have found that some of these dogs do better at holding their weight if they are fed their normal amount of dog food in two feedings instead of one.

As eating patterns can vary with Boston Terriers, you will have to experiment to see which way you can best maintain your dog's ideal weight. All Bostons, regardless of weight, need regular exercise in order to be well-muscled, alert, and in all-around good shape.

CHAPTER

6

Understanding the Boston Terrier Standard

FOLLOWING IS THE STANDARD OF THE BOSTON TERRIER. IT HAS BEEN REVISED several times in the last hundred years, always with the intention of clarifying the interpretation for exhibitors, breeders, and judges by drawing a picture in our mind of that perfect specimen of the breed.

There has been some disagreement among breeders about whether too much emphasis has been put on the head of the Boston Terrier, but this is a breed that has always placed great emphasis on the head. We know that a Boston Terrier needs much more than just the correct head, but without the correct head we cannot have a true representative of the breed. Again, this is not to say that a good head is all that a Boston Terrier needs. To the contrary, although the correct head is an absolute necessity, a true specimen must adhere to the *entire* Standard.

A good Boston must typify the personality and temperament that have made this breed a joy to live with and must move with the momentum of a sure-footed, strait-gaited dog without a paddling, crossing, or Hackney gait. The dog should possess a nice level topline ending with the rump gently rolling into the tail set. In the front the topline should flow into a gracefully arched neck, the perfect pedestal on which to display a magnificent head. The short-backed body should be mounted on a good straight front and a strong well-angulated rear.

Following is the **STANDARD OF THE BOSTON TERRIER** with drawings by Vickie Kwasny and photographs by Lisa Braunstein–La Mere and Cindy McIntosh. It was produced by the Boston Terrier Club of America, Inc., in order to help the student of the breed to understand the breed Standard.

GENERAL APPEARANCE

The Boston Terrier is a lively, highly intelligent, smooth-coated, short-headed, compactly built, short-tailed, well-balanced dog, brindle, seal or black in color and evenly marked with white. The head is in proportion to the size of the dog and the expression indicates a high degree of intelligence.

The body is rather short and well knit, the limbs strong and neatly turned, the tail is short and no feature is so prominent that the dog appears badly proportioned. The dog conveys an impression of determination, strength and activity, with style of a high order; carriage easy and graceful. A proportionate combination of "Color and White Markings" is a particularly distinctive feature of a representative specimen.

"Balance, Expression, Color, and White Markings" should be given particular consideration in determining the relative value of GENERAL APPEARANCE to other points.

SIZE, PROPORTION, SUBSTANCE

Weight is divided by classes as follows: Under 15 pounds; 15 pound and under 20 pounds; 20 pounds and not to exceed 25 pounds. The length of leg must balance with the length of body to give the Boston Terrier its striking square appearance.

Influence of Sex is a comparison of specimens of each sex; the only evident difference is a slight refinement in the bitch's conformation.

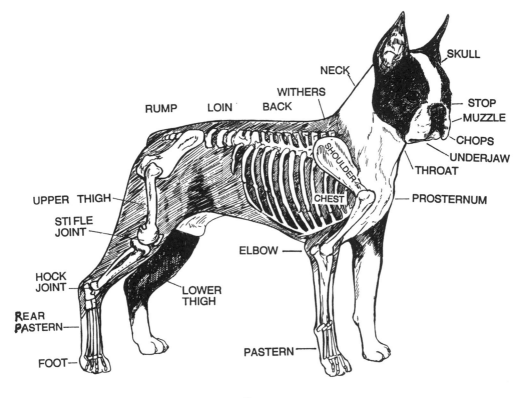

NECK

WITHERS

BACK

RUMP   LOIN

SKULL

STOP

MUZZLE

CHOPS

UNDERJAW

THROAT

SHOULDER

CHEST

PROSTERNUM

UPPER THIGH

STIFLE
JOINT

ELBOW

HOCK
JOINT

LOWER
THIGH

REAR
PASTERN

FOOT

PASTERN

Structure.

HEAD

The skull is square, flat on top, free from wrinkles, cheeks flat, brow abrupt and the stop well defined. The ideal Boston Terrier expression is alert and kind, indicating a high degree of intelligence. This is a most important characteristic of the breed. The eyes are wide apart, large and round and dark in color. The eyes are set square in the skull and the outside corners are on a line with the cheeks as viewed from the front. Disqualify: Eyes blue in color or any trace of blue. The ears are small, carried erect, either natural or cropped to conform to the shape of the head and situated as near to the corners of the skull as possible.

The muzzle is short, square, wide and deep and in proportion to the skull. It is free from wrinkles, shorter in length than in depth; not exceeding in length approximately one-third of the length of the skull. The muzzle from stop to end of the nose is parallel to the top of the skull. The nose is black and wide, with a well defined line between the nostrils. Disqualify: Dudley nose.

The jaw is broad and square with short, regular teeth. The bite is even or sufficiently undershot to square the muzzle. The chops are of good depth, but not pendulous, completely covering the teeth when the mouth is closed. Serious Fault: Wry mouth. Head Faults: Eyes showing too much white or haw. Pinched or wide nostrils. Size of ears out of proportion to the size of the head. Serious Head Faults: Any showing of the tongue or teeth when the mouth is closed.

NECK, TOPLINE AND BODY

The length of neck must display an image of balance to the total dog. It is slightly arched, carrying the head gracefully and setting neatly into the shoulders. The back is just short enough to square the body. The topline is level and the rump curves slightly to the set-on of the tail. The chest is deep with good width, ribs well sprung and carried well back to the loins. The body should appear short. The tail is set on low, short, fine and tapering, straight or screw and must not be carried above the horizontal. (Note: The preferred tail does not exceed in length more than one-quarter the distance from set-on to hock.) Disqualify: Docked tail. Body Faults: Gaily carried tail. Serious Body Faults: Roach back, sway back, slab-sided.

A good head with good width and depth of muzzle as well as correct eye and ear set.

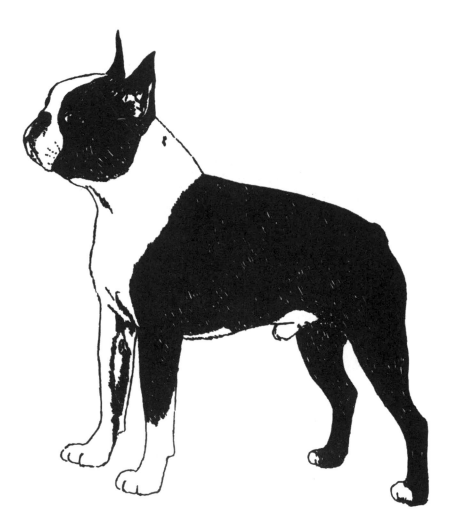

The type of Boston Terrier for which you breed. A good head on an excellent body.

FOREQUARTERS

The shoulders are sloping and well laid back, which allows for the Boston Terrier's stylish movement. The elbows stand neither in nor out. The forelegs are set moderately wide apart and on a line with the upper tip of the shoulder blades. The forelegs are straight in bone with short, strong pasterns. The dewclaws may be removed. The feet are small, round and compact, turned neither in nor out, with well-arched toes and short nails. Faults: Legs lacking in substance; splay feet.

HINDQUARTERS

The thighs are strong and well muscled, bent at the stifles and set true. The hocks are short to the feet, turning neither in nor out, with a well defined hock joint. The feet are small and compact with short nails. Fault: Straight in stifle.

GAIT

The gait of the Boston Terrier is that of a sure footed, straight gaited dog, forelegs and hind legs moving straight ahead in line with perfect rhythm, each step indicating grace and power. Gait Faults: There will be no rolling, paddling, or weaving when gaited. Hackney gait. Serious Gait Faults: Any crossing movement, either front or rear.

COAT

The coat is short, smooth, bright and fine in texture.

COLOR AND MARKINGS

Brindle, seal, or black with white markings. Brindle is preferred ONLY if all other qualities are equal. (Note: **SEAL DEFINED.** Seal appears black except it has a red cast when viewed in the sun or bright light.) Disqualify: Solid black, solid brindle or solid seal without required markings. Gray or liver colors.

Required Markings: White muzzle band, white blaze between the eyes, white-forechest.

Desired Markings: White muzzle band, even white blaze between the eyes and over the head, white collar, white forechest, white on part or whole of forelegs and hind legs below the hocks. (Note: A representative specimen should not be penalized for not possessing "Desired Markings.") A dog with a dog with a preponderance of white on the head or body must possess sufficient merit otherwise to counteract its deficiencies.

TEMPERAMENT

The Boston Terrier is a friendly and lively dog. The breed has an excellent disposition and a high degree of intelligence, which makes the Boston Terrier an incomparable companion.

SUMMARY

The clean-cut, short-backed body of the Boston Terrier, coupled with the unique characteristics of his square head and jaw, and his striking markings have resulted in a most dapper and charming American original: The Boston Terrier.

SCALE OF POINTS

General Appearance	10
Expression	10
Head (Muzzle, Jaw, Bite, Skull and Stop)	15
Eyes	5
Ears	5
Neck Topline, Body, and Tail	15
Forequarter	10
Hindquarter	10
Feet	5
Color, Coat and Markings	5
Gait	10
Total	100

DISQUALIFICATIONS

Eyes blue in color or any trace of blue.

Dudley nose.

Docked tail.

Solid black, solid brindle, or solid seal without required markings.

Gray or liver colors.

LOOKING BACK

At this point it would be interesting to look back at perhaps the earliest Standard for the breed that is now known as the Boston Terrier. This Standard was adopted when the breed was known as the Round-Headed Bull and Terrier Dog.

Skull—Large, broad, and flat.

Stop—Well defined.

Ears—Preferably cut; if left on, should be small and thin, situated as near corners of the skull as possible. Rose ears preferable.

Eyes—Wide apart, large, round, dark, and soft; not "goggle" eyed.

Muzzle—Short, round, and deep, without wrinkles; nose should be black and wide.

Mouth—Preferably even; teeth should be covered when mouth is closed.

Neck—Thick, clean, and strong.

Body—Deep at chest and well ribbed up, making a short-backed, cobby-built dog; loins and buttocks strong.

Legs—Straight and well muscled.

Feet—Strong, small, and moderately round.

Tail—Short and fine, straight or screw, carried low.

Color—Any color except black, mouse, or liver; brindle and white, brindle, or whole white are the colors most preferred.

Coat—Short, fine, bright, and hard.

Symmetry—Of a high order.

Disqualifications—Hair lip, docked tail, and any artificial means used to deceive the judge.

Weight—Dogs of different weights are divided into three classes, as follows: fifteen pounds and under, twenty-five pounds and under, and thirty-six pounds and under.

Scale of Points

Skull	15
Muzzle	15
Nose	5
Eyes	5
Ears	5
Neck	5
Body	10
Legs and feet	10
Tail	10
Color and coat	10
Symmetry	10
Total	100

Upon close comparison of the two, we can see that the current Standard no longer calls for a large skull, ears are no longer preferred cut, and rose ears are no longer in the Standard. The preferred muzzle is now square instead of round. The bite is now even or undershot, and the neck is now slightly arched and graceful instead of thick. Whole white, which was once preferred, is no longer included in the Standard, just as the twenty-six-to-thirty-five-pound class is not included.

As stated in the introduction, only time will indicate the progress of the breed. With conscientious breeders breeding *to* the Standard, the breed will be in good hands.

GLOSSARY FOR THE STANDARD

Back, *Roached*: A curvature or arch along the back.

Sway: A dip or curvature between the withers and the hip bone.

Balance: Conformation that is symmetrical and in proportion, each part blending smoothly into the next. Front and rear assemblies equal each other in angulation and reach and drive. Balance may differ according to specific breed Standard.

Bite, *Even*: Meeting of the front teeth at the edges with no overlap of the upper or lower teeth.

Overshot: The front teeth of the upper jaw overlap or project beyond the teeth of the lower jaw when the mouth is closed.

Undershot: The front teeth of the lower jaw overlap or project beyond the teeth of the upper jaw when the mouth is closed.

Blocky: Excessive width in relation to length. Square, For example, a blocky head is broader and coarser than it should be.

Chunky: A body that is too short for its length and may appear chopped off.

Coarse: Lacking in refinement, too large, too heavy.

Dudley Nose: Flesh colored nose.

Gait, *Hackney*: The high lifting of the front legs at the carpal joint like the Hackney horse. This is an abnormal movement for most breeds that requires steep shoulder angulation and wastes' energy.

Paddling: Named for the similarity to a canoeist's motion. The front feet swing forward on a stiff outward arc and circular motion with each step.

Rolling: Swaying action of the hindquarters when moving.

Weaving: An unsound gait when either the front or rear quarters (or both) cross over in front of one another.

Haw: A membrane on the inside of the eyelid; the conjunctiva.

Slab Sided: Flat ribs with too little spring.

Sloping, Well-Laid-Back Shoulders: An approximate 90 degree angle of the shoulder with the upper arm.

Spindly: When Lanky, thin, lacking bone or substance.

Well Knit: A short-coupled body with strong, well-developed muscles.

Wry Mouth: The lower jaw is twisted and does not line up with the upper jaw.

EVALUATING YOUR DOG ACCORDING TO THE STANDARD

You now may try to compare your Boston Terrier with the Standard. Evaluate your dog on a sturdy table with a piece of carpet to give safe footing. Make sure that the area is well lit with plenty of room for you to step back and judge the dog's general appearance.

Head

We will begin with the head because a Boston Terrier without the prescribed head is not a good specimen, no matter how perfect the body. Study your dog's head well. Is the head structure correct? Is the skull square and flat on top as it should be, or is the dog apple-headed with a curved skull? Does the dog have a terrier-type head and muzzle, or is the head too coarse and unrefined? It is important to remember that the square head is formed by an upper square, with the ears set as near the corners of the skull as possible. The ears are in line with the outside corner of the eyes on a line with the cheeks when viewed from the front. The lower square of the head is formed by the eye placement and the muzzle.

Expression

Next, check your Boston Terrier's expression. The Standard states that this is the most important characteristic of the breed. The ideal expression of a Boston Terrier is alert and kindly, indicating a high degree of intelligence. This expression comes not only from the Boston Terrier's large, round, dark eyes and ear set, but also from an inner attitude that lets the whole world know how special the dog is. Is the muzzle short, square, wide, and deep? Is the top of the skull parallel with the top of the muzzle?

Correct muzzle viewed from the side.

Incorrect terrier type—head weak and muzzle too long.

Coarse head on sway-backed body with splash markings and straight stifles.

Cheeky, muzzle too narrow in comparison to skull.

Correct eye, large and round with excellent expression. Muzzle in proportion, but ears too large for head.

Correct eye, ear set, and muzzle. Uncropped ears are in proportion to head and held erect.

Ears set too far back, too much white showing in eyes, narrow muzzle.

Cropped ears held erect and set in skull correctly to form a square with the eyes. Good expression.

Ears set too low, eyes too small, skull too round.

Check the bite to see that it is either even or, better yet, undershot to square the jaw. Whether cropped or natural, the ears must be in proportion to the head and well placed at the corner of the skull. Is your dog too cheeky; have a wrinkled skull; have too narrow a muzzle or too much white showing in the eyes? Check to see if the tongue or teeth show when the mouth is closed. Are the eyes too small or the head too round? Although a young Boston Terrier may have a slightly rounded skull that should flatten with maturity, some never reach the desired flatness. An apple head is one of the faults most often seen in the breed.

All the required head markings that make a Boston Terrier present? The required head markings are the white nose band and the blaze extending from the nose band up between the eyes and onto the top of the skull. These markings affect the expression and are characteristic of the breed. These markings are essential, and no Boston Terrier should be shown without them.

If your dog meets all of the above criteria in the Standard you are indeed fortunate. However, this is but one part of the standard that your dog needs to meet in order to be entirely correct.

Body

Next, we will attempt to have you check your dog's overall general appearance to back up the good head. Your Boston should be a compactly built, short-tailed, well-balanced dog with a head in proportion to body size. The Boston should be a sound, well-moving, typey dog of correct color and required markings. A dog too long in body, with too long a tail, a bad front or rear, cannot be well balanced.

Gait

At this point you need to have someone move your Boston for you so that you can see if your dog moves with determination and displays easy and graceful carriage. This is displayed in the gait, which should be that of a sure-footed, straight-gaited dog. Forelegs and hindlegs should move straight ahead in line with perfect rhythm, each step indicating grace and power. The Boston is not meant to roll or paddle or move too close in the rear. You must observe whether the feet point directly forward as they should. As the handler moves your dog toward you, look for any tendency

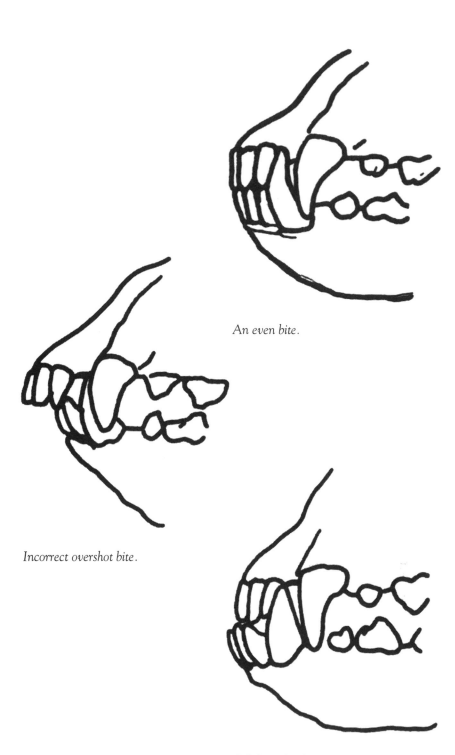

An even bite.

Incorrect overshot bite.

Slightly undershot bite.

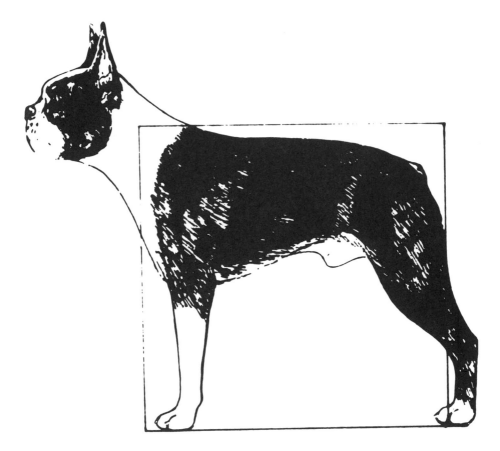

The length of leg equals the length of body.

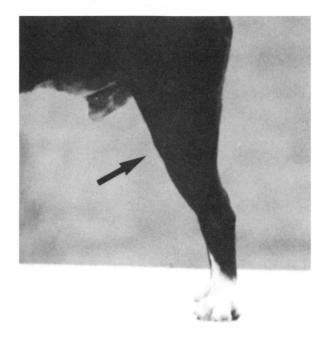

Poor rear profile, straight stifles, tail set too high and carried above topline in drawing.

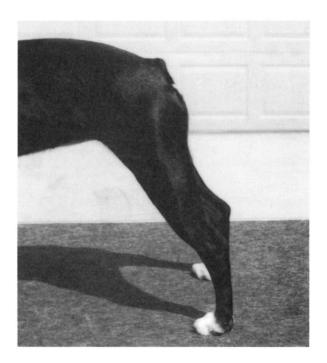

Tail set correctly.

Paddling movement.   *Good movement head on.*

to weave, cross one foot in front of the other, or throw the feet out. Weaving may indicate loose shoulders, whereas throwing the feet out may indicate too tight a shoulder.

Front Assembly

The forequarters of the Boston Terrier begin with sloping and well-laid-back shoulders. The front must be neither too narrow and close nor too wide and loaded. Check to see that your dog's elbows do not turn in or out and that the forelegs are in line with the upper tip of the shoulder blades. Your dog's legs should be straight with short strong pasterns. A Boston with weak pasterns and splayed feet cannot be a good specimen of the breed. Your Boston should have small, tight feet with arched toes to give the feeling of being up and alert.

Rear Assembly

Now have the handler move the dog away from you so that you can look for evidence of cowhocks or movement that is too close in the rear. The hind feet, like the front feet, should turn neither in nor out and should set down squarely.

Side Gait—Lateral Movement

Now, from the side, watch the Boston move. The Boston should move with a long stride, reaching ahead with the front legs and moving powerfully with the rear legs; both front and rear movement are in balance. The upper thigh should be well angulated, meeting with the lower thigh at the stifle joint. This will give a well-muscled thigh that is absolutely necessary to ensure good movement.

The hock must be short and in proportion to the thighs. A fault in the hindquarters is straight stifles, which not only detracts from the movement of the Boston but often causes a dog to be high in the rear.

Size

Undersize, proportion, and substance—the Standard does not give preference to any one size but states that the length of leg must balance the length of body to create the square appearance. Check your dog's proportions, not only in length and height but also in bone and muscle.

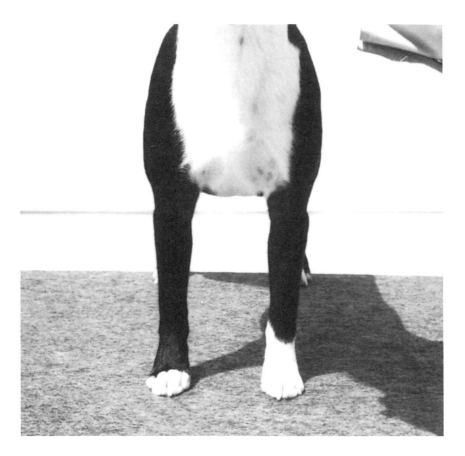

Good front, with tight feet and up on pasterns.

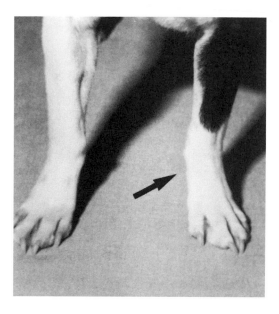

A poor front—feet turned out and down on pasterns.
Note splayed feet in photo.

Incorrect front—too wide. Note loaded sholders in photo.

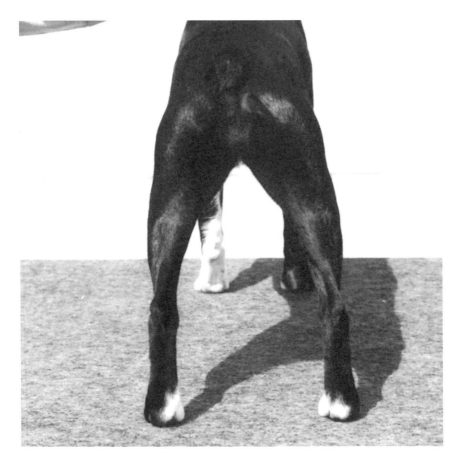

Good rear, with well-muscled, strong thighs.

Bad rear—much too wide and legs not straight.

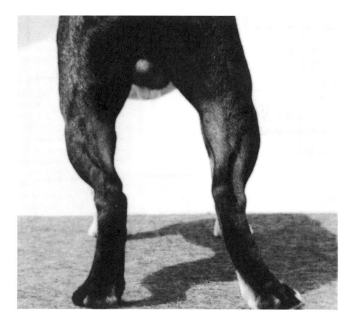

Bad rear—cowhocked and feet turned out.

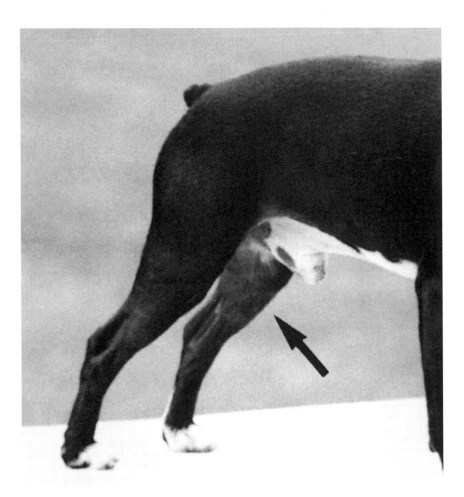

Correct hindquarters with good proportions. Note well-angulated stifle, short from hock joint to feet and strong well defined hock joint.

Level topline, good reach of front assembly.

Hackney gait.

If you have a large Boston, you must watch to see that your dog does not become too coarse or bully. A large Boston Terrier who is not overdone and is in proportion can show style and refinement. At the same time, you must watch to see that a small Boston Terrier does not develop into a spindly dog that is too refined. A small Boston who has substance and bone can compete successfully as long as it is not unusually small. The majority of show-quality Boston Terriers today seem to fall somewhere between the twelve- to twenty-pound range, but that does not mean that a smaller or larger Boston Terrier that is well balanced and true to the Standard cannot be an exceptional specimen of the breed. With that in mind, the size of your dog is of far *less* importance than balance. The Standard also allows a bitch to be slightly more refined in conformation.

Style

Does your dog have a slightly arched neck to carry the head gracefully instead of a short chunky neck? You want a neck that is in proportion to the body and one that fits neatly into well-laid-back shoulders with no dip in the withers. The neck should flow smoothly into a short, level topline that ends with a rump that is slightly curved at the set-on of the tail.

The topline should be neither roached nor swayed, although most Boston Terriers are prone to roach slightly on a cold day. Check your dog's topline either in moderate weather or in a heated area. See that the tail is not carried above the topline and is not longer than one quarter of the distance between the set-on and the tail. A docked tail is a disqualification.

Look for a deep chest with good width. The ribs should be well sprung but neither barrel chested or slab sided. If the ribs are carried well back, the loins will be short. The body should be short and compact. A short back more efficiently delivers the power of movement from the hindquarters, where it is generated. A short back also helps to square the body.

While you are examining your dog, be sure that in male dogs both testicles have descended into the scrotum. Although this is not specifically mentioned in the Standard, it is a basic requirement for all male dogs. Cryptorchidism is the failure of both testicles to descend, and monorchidism is the failure of one testicle to descend.

Too coarse or bully—thick neck, poor ear set, too much white showing around eyes.

Good length of neck with well-laid-back shoulders and good chest.

Color and Markings

Coat, color, and markings are the finishing touches for the Boston Terrier. Your dog's coat should be short, smooth, bright, and fine in texture. The condition of the coat is generally determined by the overall well-being of the dog. A dog infested with worms can hardly sport a healthy, shiny coat.

As far as color, your Boston can be one of three colors: brindle, seal, or black with white markings. You need to ascertain that your Boston is not a solid color without the required white markings, or is not a gray or liver color.

Although markings are not the most important attribute of the Boston, it is the *required* markings of a white muzzle band, blaze between the eyes, and white forechest that make a Boston look like a Boston. Without the required markings your dog cannot be a worthy show dog. The *desired* markings—a white muzzle band, an even white blaze between the eyes and over the head, a white collar, a white forechest, or white on part or the whole of forelegs and hind legs below the hocks—give the Boston that extra flashiness but are not necessary in the show dog.

You will already know whether your Boston Terrier has the friendly, intelligent disposition that is one of the most important characteristics of the breed. A shy, timid, or aggressive personality is not acceptable in a Boston Terrier.

We hope that this chapter has enabled you to evaluate your Boston Terrier critically. You need not be disappointed if your dog does not measure up to perfection as stipulated by the Standard. Few Bostons do. The perfect Boston has yet to be whelped, although many who are close to perfection have been. If your Boston Terrier possesses a glaring fault, that will not necessarily keep it from being an affectionate and loving companion. If you were considering showing or breeding your dog, at this point you would do best to find the dog a good home and begin the task of locating a Boston Terrier who better suits your goals or resolve to keep the dog as an adored pet who will be neutered.

The Boston Terrier is a particularly hard breed to evaluate as a puppy as there are so many areas in which the puppy can stray from the Standard when mature. This is also true in the area of genetic problems. In the future, new tests may be available that will help to identify carriers

Good topline.

Required markings.

Mismarked head.

Desired markings.

of unwanted recessive genes and thus help us to eliminate serious hereditary problems in Boston Terriers. With or without these new tests, it is up to responsible breeders to select breeding stock carefully so as to maintain soundness and ensure adherence to the Boston Terrier Standard.

CHAPTER

7

Do You Really
Want to Breed?

Problems within the Breed

WE ALL ENJOY THE EXPECTATION OF A LITTER OF BOSTON TERRIER PUPPIES, BUT
have we stopped to assess all the responsibilities that come with that
decision and the problems that we can encounter in breeding Boston
Terriers?

TO BREED OR NOT TO BREED

Our first responsibility is to be absolutely certain that the Boston
Terriers that we intend to breed are free from defects in structure, health,
and personality. *There is no need to breed Boston Terriers of mediocre quality.* We should always plan breedings with the goal of improving the breed.
Inferior bitches should not be bred to a better male in the hope of breeding better puppies. Only quality bitches should be bred, and they should

go to males who complement them and will improve the quality of the puppies. The ultimate goal in breeding Boston Terriers is to breed the perfect Boston Terrier or at least one that meets all the requirements of the Standard.

Many an owner of an inferior bitch has spent much time looking for a male to improve the qualities of the puppies, when in fact what they really need to do is to find a quality bitch to use for the foundation of their breeding—because no matter how good a male they use for stud, they must remember that *half the genes behind the offspring will be from the dam*. And even with the use of better quality stud dogs, it will take many, many generations before one can breed out serious faults; there is always the chance that these faults can turn up many generations later. Always remember, before you breed a prospective bitch *or* stud dog, that you are combining the genes of these Bostons to be carried forward for countless generations. Each breeding will have consequences for numerous breedings to come. The quality of Boston Terriers each of us breeds will have a direct effect upon the Boston Terriers that are sold both as pets and as show dogs. *Each breeding must be seen as being a part of the future of the breed.*

BREEDING RESPONSIBILITIES AND DIFFICULTIES

Once we have produced a litter of puppies, regardless of how good or bad, it is our responsibility to care for the mother and her pups until they have been placed in suitable homes. This entails caring for the dam, having her and her pups checked by a veterinarian, giving all required inoculations, and worming. The pups must be weaned and placed on the proper diet. They must be kept clean at all times and they must be kept well groomed. Much time must be devoted to socializing and training each individual puppy. The choice of stud dog and brood bitch to be bred determines the hereditary attributes that the puppies receive, but the amount and type of training and socialization that each puppy receives will do much to assure that it is a well-adjusted and mentally sound specimen of the breed.

Regardless of how well we plan each breeding, there is always an outside chance that the breeding will produce a sick or inferior puppy or,

Ch. Unique's Star of Zodiac, mother of Ch. Zodiac's Special Beau, bred and owned by Juanita Camp.

Ch. M L's Ace High, owned by Frank Guemple.

worse yet, having a puppy born with such a severe problem that we must decide to euthanize.

Another problem with breeding Boston Terriers is the fact that our bitches are often unable to free whelp their puppies and instead have to undergo the major surgery of the Caesarean section. The main reason why so many of our Boston Terrier bitches require a Caesarean section is due to the size of the puppies' heads in contrast to the mother's pelvic structures. The fact that Boston Terrier bitches often have only one or two large puppies, as opposed to five or six smaller puppies, also increases the frequency of the use of Caesarean section. We feel that many of these surgeries are, perhaps, unnecessary; however, as many breeders of Boston Terriers have found over the years, when one is in doubt, it is far better to elect to go with the Caesarean section and have live puppies than to let the bitch labor until one or all of the puppies are dead. Breeding Boston Terriers who require C-sections is an added expense for the breeder, and it also starts the puppy's life in a more precarious state. The dam has quite a bit of healing to do, and she is not able to care for her pups as well as she would following a normal free whelping.

Once you have your litter of Boston Terriers alive and breathing, there are still other problems to be encountered, such as a dam who either will not or cannot nurse her puppies. One of the worst problems, although quite rare, is the dam who attacks her puppies. Once a dam has demonstrated these tendencies, it is best never to breed her again, as these traits could be hereditary.

Another problem facing the Boston Terrier breeder is the Fading Puppy Syndrome. This can result from a variety of causes, such as congenital defects, infectious diseases, underdeveloped lungs, chilling, bacteria, and viruses. The Fading Puppy Syndrome can be diagnosed and treated only by a veterinarian if you are to have any chance of saving the puppy. Even with the help of a veterinarian, however, many of the puppies cannot be saved, especially if their symptoms are due to underdeveloped internal organs.

Juvenile cataracts are yet another problem to discourage a would-be Boston Terrier breeder. Fortunately, however, tests should soon be available through DNA testing to determine if a stud dog or bitch is a carrier. In the meantime, breeders can have their breeding stock certified clear and can be careful to *avoid breeding any lines that are known cataract carriers*.

CHOICES—TO BEGIN

If you have weighed all of the above-mentioned problems and you still want to breed (while realizing that breeding Boston Terriers is an expensive and *very* time-consuming proposition), you need to start by acquiring a bitch who not only has all the qualities that you want her to pass on but who also has ancestors who possessed all these qualities.

Once you have a quality bitch, you need to begin the process of finding a stud dog of sufficient merit. He *also* needs to have quality ancestors who were excellent representatives of the breed. Although breeding superior specimens of the breed can greatly increase your chance of breeding an exceptional puppy, nothing can guarantee what you will breed. Since the Standard of the Boston Terrier calls for so many difficult and contrary requirements, it is a wonder that we breed as many correct specimens as we do.

A final and most important consideration for you to think about before you breed is the prospect of placing each new puppy in a suitable home. Some puppies are near-perfect show specimens and you will have no trouble placing them in show homes, though you still need to check the reputation of the exhibitor or breeder to whom you will be selling each of these puppies.

Some of the most difficult situations that we have had are in placing puppies in pet homes. The best place for your puppy can be a loving pet home, because a Boston Terrier by nature enjoys being the entire center of attention and having the run of the house and the feeling of being a part of the family. But when you sell your puppies it is much more difficult to check out each of these pet homes. You are indeed fortunate if you can sell your puppies to friends or relatives, or if you have some knowledge of how the puppy will be treated and cared for. You are also extremely fortunate if, after years of breeding, you are able to sell a puppy to a previous buyer who has proven to be a loving, responsible dog owner. But these are not always the people who come to buy your puppies. You will have to make judgments about complete strangers as to whether they are the good, responsible dog owners to whom you want to sell your puppies. You will find yourself responsible for finding suitable homes for *every* puppy you breed. That is quite a responsibility!

We also have a responsibility to the brood bitches after we have bred them. We need to find a good pet home for them where they will be loved

Ch. Ancoramn Special Brandywine, bred and owned by Marilyn and Norman Randall of Maryland.

and cared for as part of the family, because being loved and cared for as a pet is their reward. Before placing the brood bitch it is best to have her spayed.

When we made the decision many years ago to breed Boston Terriers, we decided to have our basement remodeled to accommodate four-feet-by-eight-feet runs for our dogs. Even with runs of such a nice size for the dogs, they still need time to run in the yard in nice weather and time to take turns in the house with us. We know that this is not as ideal a situation as being a house dog all the time, but it is much better than being confined to a small kennel most of the time.

Before you breed, therefore, make sure that you have the time and space for each of your brood bitches and make sure that you will be able to screen each potential puppy buyer fully. You can learn a great deal from each buyer by discussing how he or she intends to keep, care for, and train the puppy. Many times we have had to refuse to sell our puppies to potential buyers for various reasons, such as unruly children who would be a danger to the puppy, or misinformed buyers who said they had no fenced yards and did not believe in keeping a puppy on a lead and would just train the puppy not to go out in high traffic areas, and other situations where a placement was not suitable. You will develop an instinct for judging potential buyers, but this takes a little time.

DO YOU OR DON'T YOU?

If, after careful consideration, you feel that you would really like to breed your Boston Terrier and *she is of sufficient quality and pedigree to be bred*, you must find a suitable stud dog to complement her. You are sure to find much joy in anticipation of whelping a sound and healthy Boston Terrier puppy. Although you can hope for more than one puppy, it is far better to produce one very good Boston Terrier than a large litter of average ones.

Ch. Karadin Kiss Me Kate, bred and owned by Ethel Braunstein of California.

CHAPTER

8

The Brood Bitch and the Stud Dog

YOUR CHOICE OF BROOD BITCH IS A VERY IMPORTANT STEP IN BREEDING Boston Terriers. The puppies you produce will depend on her and her ancestors *for 50 percent of their genes*, which thus determine their quality. That is why it is so important, *before* you purchase a puppy with the intent to eventually breed, that you begin by attending dog shows in your area to see what quality is available. If at all possible, it is most beneficial to the novice breeder to attend shows in several areas so as to compare the Boston Terriers that are being produced in different areas and thus be able to study the pedigrees of these Boston Terriers. You need to study the Standard so that you know what you should be looking for in type and conformation. Next, you need to study the pedigrees of the Boston Terriers and learn as much as possible about different lines. You need to talk with the breeders of the dogs that best exemplify the Standard and discuss different lines with them.

You may also be able to find a breeder or two who are producing quality Boston Terriers and who are willing to take the time to explain

Ch. El-Bo's Rudy is a Dandy, bred and owned by Bob and Eleanor Candland of California.

to you what qualities to look for in both a stud dog and a brood bitch. No one can guarantee that you will have immediate success breeding any particular lines, but you will have much better odds of breeding top-quality Boston Terrier puppies if you begin with a brood bitch who not only looks like the quality of puppy that you hope to breed but who also has a long line of quality Boston Terriers behind her.

Another aspect that you may want to consider is whether or not your bitch comes from a line of free whelpers. There is no guarantee that any brood bitch will free whelp, but you will have a slightly better chance if your brood bitch does come from a line of free whelpers.

In order to breed Boston Terriers you need to acquire only the brood bitch. You may or may not, at a later date, wish to acquire a stud dog. The best way of choosing a stud dog is by traveling to shows and seeing the dogs. You may also want to check out breed publications and catalogs to see what new dogs are available and see what kind of puppies these stud dogs are producing. It is more important to find a stud dog who is siring Bostons of exceptional quality than to breed to a stud dog that is siring average quality. As with the brood bitch, what is behind the stud dog is of the utmost importance. The genes that the stud dog transmits to your puppies are an accumulation of the genes passed on to him by his ancestors.

BREEDING STRATEGIES

There are three types of breeding: inbreeding, linebreeding, and outcrossing. **Inbreeding** involves the mating of close relatives, such as father to daughter, mother to son, brother to sister, and half-brother to half-sister. In **linebreeding**, dogs are not as closely related, but they have common ancestors such as a grandparent on either the maternal or paternal side of the pedigree. **Outcrossing** is when there are no common ancestors within the first few generations. The closer that you are breeding, the more you are doubling up both the good and the bad genes. For this reason you should never breed a closely related dog and bitch who possess the same fault.

No matter how well planned your breeding, no matter how fantastic the pedigree of both the sire and the dam, and no matter how close to the Standard both the dam and the sire are, there is still no guarantee as to the quality of the puppies you will produce. There is always a chance that a recessive gene will surfacing in the puppies you produce.

With each litter of Boston Terriers, every breeder needs to stop and think that these puppies will have a direct effect on the quality of Boston Terriers in future generations. Every puppy may not turn out to be a Specialty winner, but they should at least be good, sound healthy puppies free from congenital defects and genetically transmitted problems.

The Brood Bitch

While the pedigrees of both the brood bitch and stud dog are of great importance, don't forget that to some dog people the first rule of breeding is to breed a beautiful typey dog to a beautiful typey bitch. The one remark that we have most disliked hearing over the years is "This Boston isn't really what I want, so I will just breed him/her." These breeders don't seem to understand that the puppies they get from an inferior Boston will also be inferior. It is lucky for the breed that there are a lot of conscientious breeders who maintain a high standard of integrity in their breeding programs, as evidenced by the Boston Terriers they produce.

As a guideline in acquiring a brood bitch, it is best, as in acquiring a Boston Terrier for show, to purchase an adult. If you insist on acquiring your bitch as a puppy, you must realize that there is always a chance that she could develop faults that should cause you not to breed her at all. This is where so many people who have purchased a puppy to use for breeding have made their greatest mistake. They have gone ahead and bred a bitch even though she had developed a fault in soundness or type, only *because they had purchased her to breed*. They bred her *regardless* of any faults that she had developed. This is never in the best interest of a breeding program or a breed. In order to establish any type of worthwhile breeding program you cannot be kennel blind. You have to be willing to critique your breeding stock constantly and, as sometimes happens when a Boston Terrier develops a problem, that particular animal must be eliminated from the breeding program. Any puppies who have a serious fault or a few minor ones should be spayed or neutered before they are sold and should be sold with limited registration. The following are faults that are listed in the Boston Terrier Standard (serious faults are in italics):

Wry Mouth

Eyes showing too much white or haw

Pinched or wide nostrils

Size of ears out of proportion to the size of the head

Any showing of the tongue or teeth when the mouth is closed

Gaily carried tail

Roach back, sway back, slab-sided

Legs lacking in substance; splay feet

Straight in stifle

Rolling, paddling, or weaving when gaited

Hackney gait

Any crossing movement, either front or rear

The following are disqualifications listed in the Standard:

Eyes blue in color or any trace of blue

Dudley nose

Docked tail

Solid black, solid brindle, or solid seal without required markings

Gray or liver colors

You need not have the perfect Boston Terrier to breed, but he or she should have no glaring fault that will likely be reproduced. On the other hand, since no Boston Terriers are perfect, you can try to breed out minor imperfections by selection of the proper stud dog and blood bitch.

THE STUD DOG

Selection of the proper stud dog is half study and research and half luck. Your odds will greatly increase if you find a stud dog that (1) is a beautiful dog, (2) possesses a pedigree that has common ancestors with your bitch, and (3) has already produced Boston Terriers of above-average quality.

Ch. Magnificent Rogue, owned by the late renowned judge Joe Faigel of Michigan.

BREEDING STOCK AND THE GENES

In acquiring breeding stock, let the Standard be your guide and explicitly look for Boston Terriers that exhibit overall type in balance and proportion with no single feature standing out or appearing exaggerated. The dog should be square in head and in body. The expression should be soft, alert, and well animated. The Boston Terrier should be of medium bone with good muscle and medium station, and should have a well-arched neck.

Your breeding stock should be sound. Soundness refers to the ability of the dog to function as nature intended and includes the elements of sight, sound, smell, movement, and the ability to reproduce. Soundness is often associated only with movement and faults of gait. Any structural faults such as weak pasterns, splay feet, cow hocks, roach back, dip in the withers, and loose elbows or shoulders will detract from the soundness of the specimen.

The Boston Terrier should also be sound of mind, although temperament is something that we too often take for granted. This is an integral part of the Boston Terrier and should always be considered when breeding. You want your breeding stock to have a temperament that combines an inner presence that says "here I am" with an air of pride and self confidence that sets them apart from the others.

If, after following all the above suggestions, you breed a litter that is less than you expected, you need to reexamine your bitch's pedigree and try linebreeding in a different direction. Sometimes a dog that has produced many beautiful Boston Terriers just may not "click" with your bitch. As we said earlier, no one can guarantee a successful breeding program, as luck is as essential an ingredient as sound breeding stock.

Remember that every feature a dog has or may have is determined by the genes carried by the two reproductive cells, one from each parent. In every puppy thousands of pairs of these genes combine to produce every recognizable attribute of the puppy. These genes function in pairs, one member of each pair being contributed by the father and the other contributed by the mother. **Each parent contributes 50 percent of the offspring's genes.** The parents obtained these genes from *their* parents, who in in turn received their genes from their parents, and so on back through the generations.

Ch. Gimp's Mokena, owned by Frank Guemple.

Ch. Iowana's Sundancer, owned by Leonard Myers of Colorado.

You can never know for certain which half of any pair of genes carried by a dog or a bitch will be passed on to any one of their progeny. A dog or a bitch may contribute one characteristic to one puppy and another one to another puppy in the same litter or in different litters. The number of gene pairs is so great that there is an infinite number of combinations, which accounts for the differences in type found between two full brothers or two full sisters. In fact, whether a puppy is a male or female is determined by the genes it receives.

Dominant and Recessive

Dominant and recessive genes are the two most widely known types. Because each dog possesses genes in pairs, one gene from each parent, four possible pairs can result: two recessives, one from each parent; two dominants, one from each parent; a dominant from the mother and a recessive from the father; or a recessive from the mother and a dominant from the father. It is the combination in which both members of the gene pair are recessive that presents many of the problems in breeding Boston Terriers.

When genes for a trait are recessive, they produce the recessive attribute in the dog that carries them. When the genes are both dominant, they result in the dominant attribute. When one gene is dominant and the other gene is recessive, however, the attribute will appear dominant but will breed true only half the time. This partly explains why a dog and bitch may produce a puppy that is quite different from the parents.

If we know that both genes in a particular gene pair are dominant, we can expect a dog to produce puppies that resemble him or her for that particular trait, regardless of the other parent's traits. If the genes in a particular gene pair from *both* the stud dog and the bitch are recessive, the puppies *will* look exactly like the parents for that trait. However, a stud dog with a mixed pair of genes bred to a bitch with a mixed pair of genes may produce puppies that bear no resemblance to either parent.

Because a dog has thirty-nine pairs of chromosomes, and because each chromosome contains more than 25,000 genes, the genetic possibilities are endless. Many undesirable hereditary traits are expressed by recessive genes; such a gene can be carried through many generations of offspring, causing no problems, until it is paired with another recessive gene for the

Ch. Royale Show Man, owned by Susan Ruble and Shirley Canole.

Ch. Sabe's Gold Dust, bred and owned by Sharon Saberton of Missouri.

same trait. This is why recessive traits cannot be eliminated in one or two generations of careful breeding.

In contrast, dominant traits are clearly seen in every generation of puppies. Breeders easily recognize problems caused by dominant genes, and by choosing not to breed dogs that carry these genes they can eliminate these traits from their breeding program. For this reason, hereditary problems are more frequently due to recessive genes. Some traits that may be influenced by recessive genes include: juvenile cataracts, undescended testicles, hernias, cleft palate and harelip, malocclusion, and incorrect bite.

When you breed two dogs with a common ancestor, their offspring inherit some of the same genes from each side of the pedigree. This allows for the possibility that genes will "double up." This has a twofold result—the traits are more uniform, *but* undesirable recessive genes may come to the surface and thereby give rise to serious problems.

ONCE YOU'VE MADE THE DECISION— THE NEXT STEP

Part of the breeding preparation is for the bitch owner to choose a stud dog well in advance and to let the stud dog owner know approximately when the bitch will next be in season. Both owners need to have a clear understanding of the arrangement and the terms of the breeding.

With Boston Terriers a stud fee is much more common than a "pick of the litter" arrangement. The stud fee is usually paid at the time of the breeding, when a written certificate is presented to the bitch owner stating the dates of the breedings and usually a guarantee of a return service offered if the breeding does not take. If there is a "puppy for payment" arrangement, this should be in writing, and the age of the puppy should be agreed upon. If all arrangements are in writing, there will be no misunderstandings at a later date.

Before a dog is offered at stud, a brucellosis test should be done to determine that he is free from the disease. The owner of the stud dog should require a negative brucellosis test of each bitch coming in to be bred.

As soon as the bitch comes into season the owner of the bitch should notify the owner of the stud dog. They can then make arrangements to drive or fly the bitch to the stud dog for breeding. The bitch is best sent several days before the planned breeding so that she will have time to relax and adjust to her new surroundings before the breeding. This has proved to be a good idea for times when breeders have found that their bitches were ready to be bred a day or two sooner than their owner originally thought.

The most common reason for a breeding not taking is that the bitch was bred at the wrong time in her estrus cycle. In general, the estrus cycle lasts twenty-one days from the first sign of vaginal bleeding. The first stage is called the **proestrus** and lasts for six to nine days. In this stage the bitch has a dark bloody discharge and firm swelling of the vulva. She begins attracting males but will not accept a male. The second stage of the cycle is the **estrus** (standing heat). It lasts for six to ten days. It is during this stage that the vulva softens and the discharge color lightens. The bitch raises her vulva and becomes receptive to the male. As a general rule we breed bitches on the eleventh and thirteenth days of the cycle, unless they have been bred before or their mothers had a history of being bred early or late. **Metestrus** is the third stage of the reproductive cycle, and it begins when the bitch refuses to stand for the male.

A smear can be taken of the vaginal discharge by a veterinarian during estrus. Microscopic examination will show the changes in the number of red and white blood cells. From these changes the veterinarian can determine when the bitch can be bred. Ovulation cannot be accurately predicted by just counting days, although the bitch herself can indicate when she is ready to be bred when, as was discussed previously, her vulva softens, her color lightens, she lifts her vulva, and she will accept the male. Experienced stud dogs also know when a bitch is ready to be bred; we have seen some dogs who would have nothing to do with the bitch until the time was right. Fortunately, sperm can usually survive in the female reproductive tract for up to seventy-two hours, and on occasion for as long as a week.

THE BREEDING

The breeding should take place in the house or kennel where there is a comfortable temperature and a quiet area without too many distractions from other dogs. With Boston Terriers we prefer to have one person hold the female as the male checks to see if she is receptive. If the female is friendly, it is okay to let them loose for a short time to check each other out.

If the female is then willing to accept the male, someone should hold the bitch from the front as the male mounts her from the rear. A receptive female will raise her vulva in order for the male to enter the vagina. As the male penetrates he grasps her with his forelegs and the bulabus glandis swells and is clasped by the vulva. This swelling produces the tie and stimulates the male to ejaculate.

After the dogs are tied many people let the dog lift his hindleg over the back of the bitch and let the pair stand back to back. This is the most common practice. We, however, prefer to hold the two dogs together with the male on top until the bitch releases the male. In addition, the bitch may cry, snap, or try to pull away from the male. You need to have someone steady the bitch until the tie is over, regardless of which method you use. A tie may last from a couple of minutes to a half hour. In some cases no tie occurs. After the tie is over, the bitch should be held with her rear elevated for about twenty minutes.

Options

If for one reason or another it seems that the mating will not take place naturally, and you are certain that it is the right time for the female to be bred, it is best to proceed with an **artificial insemination**. Artificial insemination will not prevent the dog or the bitch from breeding naturally in the future. Artificial inseminations may be done by a veterinarian. Some experienced breeders may be able to do them as well.

A bitch can also be bred by having **frozen semen** shipped from a canine sperm bank to your local veterinarian. Your vet will then perform an artificial insemination with the frozen sperm. The sperm bank will give specific instructions about timing and about bringing the sperm to the exact temperature required before artificially inseminating your bitch. We have had personal experience with this procedure, as we had a puppy born from frozen sperm in 1984; we have also talked with others who have had puppies from frozen sperm. In such breedings it is most important to use a veterinarian who is experienced in thawing frozen semen.

Fresh chilled semen is another avenue for consideration if, for some reason, the bitch cannot be brought to the dog. Unlike frozen semen, the specimen is not stored; it must be delivered and used shortly after collection.

Both frozen and fresh chilled semen afford opportunities to breed bitches to stud dogs who might otherwise not be available for that "ideal" breeding.

The anticipation of breeding the perfect Boston Terrier, an elusive goal, will keep us searching for that right combination of bitch and dog. Along the way we will surely breed some very good quality Bostons, together with a few that may not be exactly what we want but that all come from somewhere in the pedigree. Breeding Boston Terriers is a real challenge, but it is so rewarding when you have made a valuable contribution to the breed.

C H A P T E R

9

Pregnancy, Whelping, and Care of the Newborn

THE GESTATION PERIOD CAN BE AN ANXIOUS TIME FOR BOTH THE PREGNANT bitch and the breeder. Proper care of the pregnant bitch is of the utmost importance in breeding healthy puppies. Records of her previous pregnancies together with those of her mother can be of great help in determining whether or not she will need a Caesarian section and when she will be ready for it. The average gestation period for a Boston Terrier is sixty-three days, but healthy puppies can arrive at any time between the fifty-ninth and the sixty-sixth day. Those born before the fifty-seventh day may not be developed enough to survive.

IS SHE OR ISN'T SHE?

Many bitches carry their puppies well up under their ribs, and this makes it difficult for the breeder to know if the breeding took. With other bitches the only question is how many puppies will they have. A bitch can be palpated between the twenty-sixth and thirty-third day of gestation by laying her on her side so that her abdomen is relaxed. Then place one hand beneath and one hand on top of her lower abdomen and gently feel for small firm lumps. A negative palpation does not completely rule out pregnancy even when performed by a veterinarian.

Other signs of pregnancy are weight gain, enlargement of the breasts and abdomen, increased appetite, morning sickness, or even a clear stringy discharge from the vulva. An ultrasound test of x-ray can be done toward the end of the pregnancy but this is not really necessary.

It is a good idea to have your bitch checked by your veterinarian not only before breeding but again a couple of weeks before her expected delivery date to check for any possible delivery problems. You may also ask if your vet wants to schedule a C-section should she not be able to free whelp. At this time you can also discuss care of the newborn. Always have a phone number where you can reach your vet in case of emergency, along with the number of another veterinarian should yours be unavailable or out of town.

IF SHE IS. . .

During the first four weeks of pregnancy, feed your bitch her normal amount. If a bitch suffers from morning sickness, it normally lasts but a few days and is of no serious concern to you. However, you should feed your bitch several small meals spaced throughout the day, without increasing the amount. During the second half of her pregnancy increase her ration by 50 percent. At this time you also need to feed her several small meals a day. A bitch may lose her appetite a week or so before she whelps, due to her abdomen being crowded with puppies.

Do not give your bitch any medication during pregnancy without checking with your veterinarian. Your bitch should have received all her vaccinations and worming prior to breeding.

WHEN IT'S TIME

Bitches should deliver their puppies at home, where they feel secure; this may not be possible if a C-section is necessary.

If you are fortunate enough to have a free whelper, you will need a whelping box that is approximately three feet by four feet in diameter, with sides that are high enough to keep the puppies from falling out but not too high for the mother to step over. By nailing four-inch-wide boards a few inches from the floor of the box around the insides, a ledge can be built to protect the puppies from being accidentally injured by their mother. The box should be lined with towels to give the mother good traction. If you cannot construct a whelping box, a child's wading pool is an ideal substitute. The mother should be introduced to her whelping box several weeks before she is to deliver. You will also need a small box with either a hot water bottle or a heating pad under a towel at the bottom of the box, or which to place the puppies as they are delivered. Other items that you will need are:

- a small bulb syringe to remove fluids from the puppies' mouths;
- scissors;
- clean towels;
- forceps to clamp the umbilical cords;
- cotton thread to tie the cords.

Your bitch may experience loss of appetite, and restlessness several days before her due date. We have found that none of our bitches have ever eaten on the day they went into labor. Eight to twelve hours before she goes into labor, the bitch's rectal temperature may drop to 99 degrees F or below. However, normal temperature does *not* mean that she will not whelp within the next few hours.

The Whelping

The early signs of labor are panting, straining, and maybe vomiting. Some bitches squat and strain with each contraction, and others just lie down and do nothing.

In a normal delivery, the puppy is moved from the horn of the uterus to the birth canal, and is usually presented head first. The water bag (sac) around the puppy can sometimes be seen bulging from the vagina. As the bitch has contractions, the water bag will usually burst and the puppy will be delivered shortly afterwards. Should you have a puppy that seems to be stuck, you can help the mother deliver it by gently tugging on the whelp's body when the mother has a contraction. Hold the puppy with a towel and use firm but gentle pressure when the mother contracts; do not apply pressure when the mother is not contracting.

If the mother seems to be in distress, call your veterinarian right away. Do not delay as you could lose a puppy.

After the blocky head of the Boston Terrier puppy is delivered, the body is easily delivered. The mother then instinctively removes the amniotic sac so the puppy can breathe, but sometimes you may have to tear open the sac, beginning with the area near the puppy's mouth; normally, however, the mother will start to clean the puppy automatically. She will then sever the umbilical cord and begin to lick the puppy. Next she should deliver the placenta, which should be delivered within a few minutes of each puppy. Always make sure that there is one placenta delivered for each puppy, as a retained placenta can cause a serious postnatal infection known as acute metritis. She may also try to eat the placenta, but it is best not to allow her to eat all of them as they may upset her digestive tract. Eating some of them is recommended, however, as they provide nutrients and stimulate milk production. If the mother does not sever the umbilical cord, you need to cut it with sterile scissors, tie it off with thread, and apply a drop of iodine to it.

After each puppy is born there is usually a time of rest for the mother. This time can last from just a few minutes to several hours.

You should use the bulb syringe to aspirate fluids from the puppy's mouth. Rub the puppy briskly with a towel. If fluids are still keeping the puppy from breathing, you may need to hold the puppy in your hands while gently supporting the head and then swing the puppy in a downward curve with the head at the lowest point to sling the mucus from its nostrils. If the puppy still is not breathing, gently breathe into its mouth and nostrils, being careful not to rupture the lungs by breathing too forcefully. Repeat this several times to start the puppy breathing.

It is best to move each newborn puppy to a warm, dry box lined with a towel and out of the way of drafts. This is to keep the mother from walking or rolling on the puppies during delivery. After the bitch has completed her delivery the puppies can be returned to the whelping box and put on the mother's breasts to nurse. You need to watch to make sure that all of the puppies have nursed well in the first six hours. The puppies need to be checked carefully to make sure that none have hairlips or cleft palates, in which case they should be euthanized. Mismarked puppies can be sold as pets with limited registration. These dogs should be spayed and neutered.

Whelping Difficulties

Some bitches experience difficulty in labor as their uterus does not have enough strength to expel the puppy. The uterus may respond to an injection of oxytocin from a veterinarian.

Due to their anatomical make-up, Boston Terriers are prone to whelping difficulties. Although we agree that a normal whelping is best for both the bitch and the puppies, in the past we have lost large puppies that were stuck in the birth canal, so we always take our bitches to the veterinarian for a Caesarean section as soon as labor commences. Many veterinarians perform this surgery under general anesthesia, but we prefer to have our vet administer Demeral intravenously for sedation that lasts fifty to sixty minutes and then administer 2 percent Lidocaine locally to anesthetize the incision site. We feel that this procedure is best method of Caesarean section for the mother, and it does not have the effect on the puppies that a general anesthetic does. Therefore, you start out not only with a much more alert mother but also with more alert and active puppies.

Boston Terriers seem to be predisposed to **dystocia**, a term for a difficult birth due to the large head and shoulders of the fetus. This is compounded in the case of small litters, in which the puppies have a tendency to grow too large.

After whelping, some bitches go into a convulsive paralysis known as **eclampsia.** This is more common in bitches who have not received adequate calcium during their pregnancy, but it is also possible in bitches that shed their calcium during pregnancy. The treatment for eclampsia is intravenous calcium administered by a veterinarian.

THE NEWBORNS

In most cases the mother will be able to nurse her puppies, but if a bitch is ill, you may need to place the puppies on a foster mother to nurse. This need not be a Boston Terrier. She should be of a size appropriate for Boston Terrier puppies and should be removed from her own puppies. She should accept the puppies with little difficulty. If no foster mother is available and you have an extreme emergency, it will be necessary to bottle feed or tube feed the puppies. Of the two, tube feeding is the better choice; with bottle feeding, the puppies may aspirate the formula into their lungs.

This dam is nursing a litter of healthy Boston Terrier puppies.

The following formula was given to us by our veterinarian and has been quite successful.

ORPHAN PUPPY FORMULA
    8 ounces canned evaporated milk
    8 ounces water
    8 ounces plain yogurt
    1 egg yolk
    1 jar strained baby beef (baby food)
    1 tsp. Karo syrup or honey

Mix in blender and refrigerate. The formula will keep for seventy-two hours in the refrigerator. Total amount to feed is 6cc per ounce of body weight per day, divided into four to six feedings.

Puppies may be fed by spoon or **eyedropper** as an emergency measure in the absence of a puppy nurser or tube feeder. However, you must be careful that the puppies do not choke when the formula is dropped into their mouths, as the formula can possibly be aspirated into the lungs.

The **puppy nursing bottle** has the advantage of satisfying the sucking urge, but it requires that the puppy be strong enough to suck on the nipple. You will probably need to enlarge the hole in the rubber nipple so that the milk will slowly drip out when the bottle is inverted. If the milk comes out too slowly, the puppy will tire before getting enough formula.

Warm the formula to about 100 degrees F. It will be slightly warm on your wrist, like a baby's formula. To bottle feed, the puppy should be placed stomach down. Open the whelp mouth, insert the nipple, and hold the bottle at a 45 degree angle. Keep the bottle at this angle to prevent air from getting into the puppy's stomach. By keeping a slight pull on the bottle you will encourage a pup to suck vigorously. When the pup is done eating, you will need to burp it gently.

Tube feeding has several advantages: It takes about two minutes to perform each feeding; no air is swallowed and no burping is required; it ensures that you administer the proper amount of formula to each puppy; and it is the only possible method of nursing sick puppies who are too weak to nurse. Tube feeding is not difficult, and it can be learned in a few minutes. It requires a soft rubber catheter and a syringe that can be purchased from your veterinarian. If formula is given too rapidly or if too much is injected, it can be regurgitated. This can lead to aspiration of formula and pneumonia. Care should be taken to compute the correct amount of formula and slowly inject the formula into the tube.

The puppy's stomach is located at the level of the last rib. Measure the tube from the mouth to the last rib and mark the tube with a piece of tape. Draw the formula into the syringe and then warm it to body temperature by placing it in hot water. Moisten the tube with formula, open the puppy's mouth, and pass the tube slowly over its tongue and down its throat. The tube is too large to enter the windpipe, so there is little danger of passing it the wrong way. Use gentle pressure to get the puppy to swallow the tube. Insert the tube until it reaches the level of the mark or when resistance is met. Connect the syringe to the tube and slowly inject the formula into the puppy's stomach. Continue this over the first two weeks of the puppy's life; then change to a larger tube, as the smaller tube may now accidentally go down the windpipe. If the tube does go into the windpipe, the puppy will choke and cough. By this time, the puppy may be strong enough to suck from a bottle.

Both overfeeding and underfeeding are common problems with caring for orphan puppies. If your puppy is gaining weight, seems content, and has a firm yellow stool, you can be reasonably certain that you are feeding the right amount. A puppy who is not getting enough formula will cry all day, will be listless, and will gain little or no weight. This should improve with an increase or supplementation in formula, but it is wise to determine first that there is no other cause for these symptoms before proceeding.

Most people are more likely to overfeed than underfeed. This will produce diarrhea of a greenish color caused by unabsorbed bile. You will need to cut back the size of the feedings and administer one or two cc of Milk of Magnesia. Overfeeding can also lead to depletion of the digestive enzymes and cause a gray stool that looks like curdled milk. At this point the puppy rapidly dehydrates. You will need to dilute the formula with one third water and administer Milk of Magnesia every three hours.

Dehydration is corrected by giving Pedialyte to replace electrolytes. One half cc per ounce of body weight should be given every hour by bottle or stomach tube. Severe dehydration is best treated by a veterinarian, who injects electrolytes under the skin. We once successfully treated a puppy with this condition when our veterinarian-sent us home with quite a few syringes filled with electrolytes for us to inject every few hours. The electrolytes form a large bubble under the skin, which you should gently massage until it is absorbed by the puppy.

If you are tube feeding puppies, you will need to separate them from each other to keep them from sucking each other's ears and genitalia. You can do this by dividing a cardboard box into separate compartments so that each puppy will have its own compartment. An overhead heat lamp can be used to provide warmth. A thermometer should be placed in or very near the box to monitor the temperature. Keep the temperature at 85 to 90 degrees F for the first week. During the second week reduce it to 80 to 85 degrees, and then reduce the temperature gradually to 75 degrees by the fourth week.

Healthy puppies are round and firm. They nurse vigorously and compete with their littermates for their mother's nipples. If you insert your finger into a puppy's mouth, it has a strong vigorous suckle. They are warm, their color is good, and they have a good pink muzzle. When the skin is pinched it springs back into place. When you pick up the puppy it wiggles in your hand. When you move puppies from their mother, they crawl right back to her. Newborn puppies pile up together for warmth. Healthy puppies seldom cry; crying indicates that a puppy is cold, hungry, or in pain.

Sick puppies present a completely different picture. Sick puppies feel cold and limp when picked up. They show no interest in nursing, and instead they crawl around looking for help and they fall asleep when away from the warmth of their mother and littermates. They lie with their necks bent to the side. They have a piercing cry that sometimes continues for twenty minutes or more. Their body temperature is lower than it should be, and their breathing rate is often less than ten breaths per minute. These puppies are often dehydrated. They are weak and have poor color, and when you pinch their skin it does not spring back. These puppies are often rejected by the mother, who senses that they are not going to survive and so pushes them away rather than waste her time. If a puppy is treated and the body temperature comes back to normal, the mother will accept that pup once again.

The first ten days of a puppy's life are the most critical. It is extremely important that puppies in this age bracket be kept from chilling. A puppy's survival depends largely on the warmth of its surroundings, since a pup's temperature does not reach 101 degrees before four weeks. Puppies must be kept in a very warm, dry area that is free from drafts. Make sure that the dam is not wet when she comes in from the outside, as this can chill the puppies. Keep a close watch on the puppies during the first few days to make sure that none of them gets stranded in a corner. If this happens, the puppy's body temperature can drop very quickly, and this can lead to a chilled puppy. A puppy who is limp and cold is in serious trouble, and it must be warmed immediately but gradually. Never use a heating pad for a chilled puppy. Rapid warming causes dilation of the skin vessels, causing increased loss of heat. The best way to warm chilled puppies is to tuck them under a sweater or jacket next to your skin to let your warmth gradually warm the pup. You can also use a plastic bottle filled with hot water and wrapped in a towel so as not to burn the pup. The water must be changed regularly as it begins to cool and further chills the puppy. If the puppy also seems to have an empty stomach, tube feed while warming it. When your pup seems to be doing better, it can be returned to the mother. In the meantime, the hot water bottle works well in a small box lined with a towel to retain heat.

It is important to remember that puppies must eliminate. If the mother is not stimulating the puppies to eliminate, you must take over. Use a cotton ball moistened with warm water and massage their abdomen and perianal area after each feeding. The mother may later take over this chore.

Puppies should gain one to one and a half grams of weight per day for each pound of anticipated size as an adult. The birth weight should be doubled in eight to ten days. Use the mother's weight to estimate the adult weight. A steady gain in weight is the best indication that the puppies are thriving. A puppy who is not gaining weight should be checked for the cause. Puppies should be weighed on a gram scale at twelve and twenty-four hours daily for the first two weeks and then every three days until they are one month old. If more than one puppy in the litter is not gaining weight, this could indicate a problem with the mother's milk, such as acid milk or inadequate milk supply. Acid milk is not likely to occur if the mother has received proper nutrition during her pregnancy.

ODDS AND ENDS—FACTS TO KNOW

Newborn puppies have heart rates of 160 beats per minute. During the first two weeks their temperature ranges from 94 to 97 degrees and during this time most of their body heat comes from the mother. The puppies' eyes and ears are sealed at birth and open at around ten days of age. Puppies are sight and sound oriented at approximately twenty-five days. Puppies first stand at approximately 15 days, and they begin to walk at twenty-one days. The early eye color of a Boston puppy is not a true indication of the later eye color.

The puppy's dewclaws will need to be removed at three to five days of age; this can be done by your veterinarian. The puppy's nails will soon begin to grow and will need to be trimmed with small manicure scissors periodically to keep them from injuring the mother. This will also keep her from beginning to wean her puppies too soon. She should be encouraged to nurse her puppies until five weeks of age, as the mother's milk is the best nutrition they can possibly receive.

During the first three weeks, healthy puppies sleep 90 percent of the time and eat about 10 percent of the time. They nurse vigorously and compete with littermates for a nipple. While sleeping, puppies jerk, kick, and whimper. This is normal and is the newborn puppy's only means of exercise. It also helps in the development of muscles.

The best things you can do at this stage are to handle the newborn Boston puppy no more than necessary and to entrust its care to the mother; she knows instinctively how to care for her puppies, stimulating them to eliminate, keeping them clean and warm, and supplying all necessary nutrition.

Good nutrition as well as good breeding is obvious in this litter of two, bred and raised by Ola Jeanne McCollough.

CHAPTER

10

Nutritional Needs

KNOWLEDGE IN THE AREA OF NUTRITION AND DIET HAS INCREASED GREATLY IN the last several decades. This new knowledge has enabled us to improve our own health and physical well-being and to increase our life span. Much of this new information has also been useful when applied to feeding dogs and puppies. They, too, can lead healthier and longer lives—which is the best reason for proper nutrition.

A carefully planned diet, together with regular exercise, will put your dog on the road to a long and healthy life. Proper nutrition must begin with the puppy in order to develop strong bone, well-conditioned muscles, and maximum natural immunity to disease and infections.

The dog's overall appearance is also related to the quality of the diet. A well-nourished, healthy dog will have a smooth, bright, healthy-looking coat. Eyes will be clear and alert. Limbs and body will be well muscled and sleek, and the dog will be neither too thin nor overweight. The dog that possesses all of the above indicators of good health is a joy, getting the best out of life and being filled with energy to romp. He will be sound and healthy.

The components of proper feeding are quality and quantity. Quality means that the food must contain all of the required body building nutrients. Quantity is the amount of food that your dog should be fed depending on size and general activity.

BASIC NUTRIENTS

The basic requirements for your dog's nutritional needs are proteins, fats, carbohydrates, vitamins, and minerals. The dog's body must satisfy a need for body-building **protein** with an adequate supply of animal and vegetable protein. You can check the percentage of protein in the dog food you are using by reading the analysis on the back of the food bag. **Fats** supply essential fatty acids needed for adequate nutrition and normal health of the dog. They furnish a concentrated source of energy and are essential components of all body cells. It is not known if dogs require a specific level of **carbohydrates** in their diets, but the basic role of carbohydrates is as a source of calories for energy. A lack of carbohydrates in the diet can lead to loose stools, diarrhea, and illness.

Vitamins are nutritional factors that are essential to the health of your dog. Those that are important to your dog are as follows:

Vitamin A is found primarily in milk, fat, liver, and liver oil. It has at least three important functions: night vision, maintaining the structure of moist membranes and body linings, and proper growth of bones. Lack of Vitamin A in the diet may cause infections in the eyes and respiratory system, retarded growth, malformed teeth, skin lesions, and possible defects in puppies.

Vitamin D is essential for the normal growth of bones and teeth. Lack of Vitamin D can result in bowed legs, bone defects, and malformed chests and skulls, and it is a major cause of rickets in dogs.

Vitamin E is needed for normal reproduction in dogs. Symptoms of deficiency are small litters, failure for breedings to take, miscarriages, and paralysis.

Vitamin K primarily prevents excessive bleeding in animals. Without Vitamin K, clotting is reduced.

Vitamin B (Thiamine) promotes growth and aids in the digestion of food. It is very important in the digestion of carbohydrates.

There are about fifteen minerals that are necessary, most of which are readily available in your dog's diet. The most vital are calcium and phosphorus, which are needed to build healthy bones and teeth. A lack of *copper* leads to anemia. *Iron* is needed to build the blood. *Iodine* prevents enlargement of the thyroid.

There are many good brands of dog food on the market that contain all the essential nutrients for your dog. Go to your petfood store, read the labels, choose one that contains all the essential ingredients, and stick to it. Frequent changes in diet cause upset stomach and other digestive imbalances.

We prefer a kibble or food that has either lamb or chicken listed as the first ingredient. Most Boston Terriers seem to enjoy having a couple of tablespoons of a good quality canned dog food or, better yet, some chicken, beef, kidney, or liver mixed in with their dry meal dog food.

EXTRAS AND BASICS

Vegetables can be added to your dog's diet. Carrots, spinach, turnip greens, beets, and cabbage add variety, and they supply vitamins and minerals. Potatoes can be fed if they are cooked and are in small quantities. Eggs and fish are excellent if cooked. *Be sure to examine fish for bones.* Meat is always a valuable addition to your dog's meal. Liver and kidney are exceptionally good because they are rich in vitamins and minerals as well as protein.

Your dog's nutritional needs are much different than yours. That is why table scraps are not the answer to a dog's nutritional requirement, although some table scraps may be included in the daily menu.

Your Boston Terrier should be fed in the same place at the same time each day with plenty of fresh water always available.

FEEDING PUPPIES AND YOUNG DOGS

Boston Terrier puppies need a lot of food, but since their stomachs are not very large, they require at least four feedings a day during the first few months. You will have to adjust the amount of food according to how much the puppy actually eats. If your pup is eating all the food, try to increase the amount. If the pup is leaving food of every meal, decrease portions until the dog's appetite increases. If a dog is regularly refusing one meals, eliminate that feeding and increase the size of the other feedings. As the Boston matures, stomach capacity will increase as the puppy is gradually cut back to three, two, and eventually one meal a day.

There are numerous good puppy foods that can be fed to a Boston Terrier puppy. And as with feeding the adult dog, most breeders choose to feed a dry puppy meal moistened with water and mixed with a good quality canned dog food.

BROOD BITCHES

The brood bitch will require more nourishment during pregnancy and while nursing puppies than at any other time. Her intake of food will increase, but as her whelps grow, her capacity to hold food decreases and she will need to be fed smaller meals more often. The brood bitch requires larger amounts of protein, calcium, vitamins, and minerals to ensure that she has healthy, well-developed puppies. For this reason, you will want to supplement her diet with meat and *cooked* eggs. Feeding cottage cheese or evaporated milk during pregnancy is good for both mother and puppies.

STUD DOGS

The stud dog should be fed the nutritional requirements of the adult dog with some extra meat in the diet. This can be either cooked or canned meat. The amount of food should be the same as for any other adult Boston, taking care that the dog does not become too fat or too thin. Regular daily exercise also needed. Stud dogs should be fed after the breeding, so that the excitement will not hamper digestion.

OVERWEIGHT DOGS

The overweight dog needs all the protein, fat, carbohydrates, vitamins, and minerals just that any other dog needs, but with fewer calories. Today there are many "lite" or reduced-calorie foods on the market. In addition to feeding a "lite" dog food, it is essential that your overweight dog get proper exercise in order to shed excess weight.

Ch. Startime's Galaxy Starbaby, owned by Dr. and Mrs. Allen E. Spinner of Florida. She shows a lovely mature bloom resulting from a nutritionally sound diet.

THE SENIOR DOG

The senior dog's digestive system is less efficient than it was when the dog was in the prime of life.

Nutritional needs reflect a different balance, and the dog can no longer process or metabolize the quantity of food per serving as in the past. For this reason, it is sometimes beneficial to feed an older dog two or three small meals a day. This seems to lessen the burden on the digestive system.

CHAPTER

11

Common Medical Problems and Related Surgeries

SINCE THE BOSTON TERRIER IS A BRACHYCEPHALIC BREED, THAT IS, A DOG THAT possesses a short muzzle or pushed-in face, some Boston Terriers may show some degree of airway obstruction that can manifest itself through snoring and snorting. This is because the dog has an elongated soft palate. This breathing difficulty is more pronounced when the dog is hot or during exercise. Puppies sometimes exhibit signs of noisy breathing, but they outgrow this condition as their head develops. If the problem remains and is very pronounced, the dog may require surgery to correct the problem. The veterinarian removes a small section of the elongated soft palate that is blocking the airway to restore normal breathing.

   The Caesarean section is the most common surgery today for Boston Terriers. As in the human population, there are probably some unnecessary Caesarean sections performed although many of them *are* quite necessary. Our veterinarian feels that if you wait until the bitch goes into labor, the placenta has already pulled away from the uterine wall and the puppies are ready to be delivered. The only free whelper we had whelped

Fig. 1

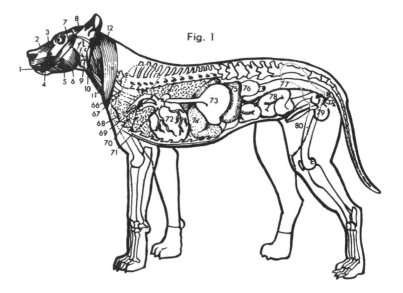

Fig. 2

Fig. 1

1 Orbicularis oris.
2 Levator nasolabialis.
3 Levator labii superioris proprius (levator of upper lip).
4 Dilator naris lateralis.
5 Zygomaticus.
6 Masseter (large and well developed in the dog).
7 Scutularis.
8 Parotid Gland.
9 Submaxillary Gland.
10 Parotido-auricularis.
11 Sterno-hyoideus.
12 Brachio-cephalicus.

(Between figures 8 and 12 on top the Elevator and Depressor muscles of the ear are to be seen.)

66 Œsophagus (gullet).
67 Trachea (wind pipe).
68 Left Carotid Artery.
69 Anterior Aorta.
70 Lungs.
71 Posterior Aorta.
72 Heart.
73 Stomach.

74 Liver. (The line in front of Liver shows the Diaphragm separating Thoracic from Abdominal cavity.)
75 Spleen.
76 Kidney (left).
77 Rectum.
77A Anal Glands (position) just inside rectum.
78 Intestine.
79 Testicle.
80 Penis.
(Midway between 76 and 79 is the seat of the Bladder and behind this the seat of the Prostate gland in males, uterus in females.)

Fig. 2

Section of Head and Neck.
1 Nasal septum.
2 Tongue.
3 Cerebrum.
4 Cerebellum.
5 Medulla oblongata.
6 Spinal Cord.
7 Œsophagus (gullet).
8 Trachea (wind pipe).
9 Hard palate.
10 Soft palate.
11 Larynx, containing vocal cords.

Internal view of a dog.

her first puppy at the veterinarian's office while he was preparing to give her an atropine shot. He had to take an emergency phone call, and when he returned she had free whelped her first puppy in that litter and went on to free whelp other litters.

We do not recommend using a veterinarian who uses a general anesthetic for a Caesarean section. We prefer to make an appointment with a vet in advance to discuss the type of procedure used for a Caesarean section. We are finding that more and more veterinarians now use a Demerol injection to sedate the bitch and then inject 2 percent Lidocaine locally into the incision site. We prefer this type of anesthetic to a general anesthetic, as the mother is more alert and better able to care for her puppies afterward. Additionally the puppies are more alert than when delivered under general anesthetic.

Dewclaws need to be removed on all Boston Terrier puppies. This can either be done by your veterinarian or you can do it yourself at home. Under the supervision of an experienced breeder with knowledge of the procedure. They need to be removed when the newborn is between three and seven days old. Waiting longer than this makes it necessary to have it done by a veterinarian, as a stitch may be necessary.

This procedure is easily done by first cleaning the area with an alcohol-soaked cotton ball and then firmly removing the dewclaw with small, sterile scissors or nipper. Cut the dewclaw off at the base, cutting slightly below skin level where the base is attached. Immediately apply styptic powder to the incision and place pressure on the incision to stop any bleeding. Watch the puppies for awhile afterward to be sure that there is no additional bleeding that you need to stop. If you ever acquire a puppy that did not have the dewclaws removed, your veterinarian can remove them at any time under anesthetic.

Owners who do not want their Boston bitches to produce puppies, do not wish to deal with messy heat cycles twice a year, and do not want to have to keep their bitches away from males during the heat cycle, can easily take care of all of that by having the bitch spayed. **Spaying** is the operation in which the uterus, tubes, and ovaries are removed. A spayed bitch will not contract pyometra and is less likely to get breast cancer. A *bitch does not need to produce a litter of puppies before she is spayed.* The best time to spay a bitch is at six months, before she goes through her first heat. *If she is not overfed and is properly exercised, she will not become fat and lethargic after being spayed.*

139

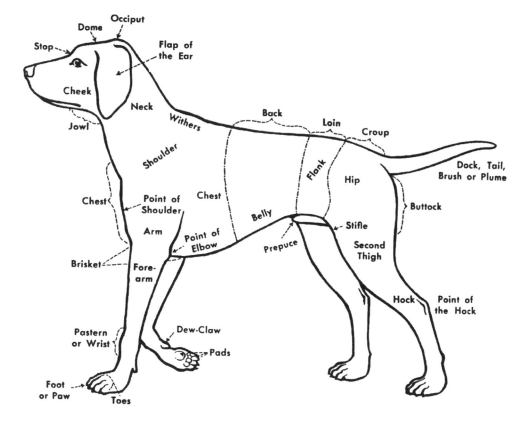

Parts of a dog.

A good time for a breeder to have a bitch spayed is while she is having a Caesarean section. This eliminates the need to have her put under anesthetic again. Having her spayed in no way interferes with her ability to nurse and care for her puppies.

Pyometra is an abcess of the uterus that occurs most frequently in females usually over five years of age. It is frequently life threatening. Its onset appears one to twelve weeks after the bitch goes out of season. Symptoms of pyometra are refusal to eat, depression, lethargy, increased thirst, and frequent urination. Often there is abdominal enlargement accompanied by either low grade or below normal temperature. Sometimes the cervix relaxes, draining a large amount of pus. Other times pus collects in the uterus, causing an enlargement of the uterus that produces painful swelling in the lower abdomen. In order to save the life of the bitch, it is best to have the veterinarian do a spay immediately, as it is better to operate on a dog without toxemia. Occasionally it is possible to treat pyometra by scraping the uterus and administering antibiotics, but this treatment is not always successful.

Distemper is a disease caused by an airborne virus and is the number-one killer of dogs. Your Boston Terrier puppies should receive distemper immunizations at an early age, and booster shots should be given annually to assure maximum protection. Symptoms of distemper are varied and may include one or a combination of several of the following: eye and nose discharge, coughing, listlessness, lack of appetite, high temperature, diarrhea, and excessive thirst. Distemper frequently affects the brain and nervous system. It lowers resistance making the dog extremely susceptible to other diseases such as pneumonia.

Leptospirosis is a disease of the kidneys caused by bacteria that are spread through the urine of dogs and the urine and droppings of rodents. As with distemper, puppies can be inoculated at an early age against leptospirosis. Symptoms include orange-colored and strong-smelling urine, dehydration, fever, vomiting, pain in the kidney area, and jaundice of the skin and eyes. Even if the disease is not fatal, the dog will probably suffer from kidney disease for the rest of its life.

Canine Parvo Virus is one of the most serious diseases and can best be prevented by vaccinating your puppy early and making sure that the last booster is given no sooner than 16 weeks of age. Parvo Virus causes violent diarrhea, sometimes bloody, and also vomiting that can quickly cause dehydration and death. This disease must be treated immediately by your veterinarian who can administer fluids to reverse the dehydration and medications to stop the diarrhea and vomiting.

Canine Corona Virus is similar to Canine Parvo Virus, and your puppy should also be vaccinated to prevent this disease. As with Parvo Virus, your puppy can quickly dehydrate from loss of fluids due to vomiting and diarrhea. This disease can sometimes run a mild course from which the puppy can quickly recover. Nevertheless, your puppy should be taken immediately to your veterinarian for the necessary treatment.

Anal gland problems can begin as mild. Your Boston scoots across the floor to put pressure on the anal glands to express some of the matter, thus relieving pressure. A severe case, in which the anal glands are infected and/or abessed, needs a veterinarian to lance and express the anal glands and start the dog on antibiotics. To empty the anal sacs you draw down on the skin at the lower part of the anus. You can feel the sacs as small, firm lumps at the five o'clock and seven o'clock positions. Grasp the perianal skin surrounding the sac with your thumb and forefinger, push in, and squeeze together. As you squeeze the sac you will express secretions with a pungent odor, which you can wipe off with a damp cloth. If there is any blood or pus in the secretions you will need to pack the anal sac with an antibiotic preparation such as Panalog by inserting the tip of the tube into the opening of the ducts. This packing process should be repeated again in two days.

If the dog has swelling at the anal gland, this is a sign of an abscessed anal sac. The abscess starts out red and later turns purple. If this occurs you will need to have your veterinarian lance the abscess to drain out the blood and pus. The abscess must heal from the inside out. The cavity should be flushed twice a day with a peroxide solution. Some dogs that have frequent anal gland infections may require surgical removal of the anal glands.

Fleas are one of the most common problems for all Boston Terriers, although they are luckier than the coated breeds as fleas can be seen more easily. There are numerous shampoos, sprays, dips, and collars available to kill fleas on your Boston.

You will also need to treat your home and yard in order to keep your Boston from being reinfested with the fleas. Fleas carry tape worm eggs with which they can infest your Boston. Check with your veterinarian to see which products to use on your Boston. We do not particularly like either sprays or collars and tend to use a flea shampoo that works quite well in our geographic area where fleas are not too great a problem. In some areas where fleas are a much greater problem, however, they need to be treated more aggressively; you should check with your veterinarian about what is the best product to use.

Some Boston Terriers are allergic to fleas and break out in a rash; they need to be treated with cortisone to block the allergic reaction and relieve the itch. **Flea allergy dermatitis** can eventually cause the skin to get thick and pigmented and the hair to fall out.

There are several varieties of **ticks,** all of which are capable of transmitting disease. The most common is the brown dog tick. The adult female tick attaches to and feeds on the dog. The tick may swell up and become the size of a pea.

Ticks are usually found on the dog's ears, head, and neck, and between the toes. When the dog has just a few ticks, you can simply remove them. Apply alcohol or nail polish remover to the tick with a cotton swab to kill it. Allow a few moments for the alcohol to work and grasp the dead tick as close as possible to the dog's skin and pull until the dead tick releases its hold. If the head remains attached to the skin, this causes only a minor reaction that clears up in a few days. Fortunately, ticks are large enough to be detected and can be found quite easily on a Boston Terrier.

Roundworms do not cause much difficulty in adult dogs, but a severe infestation in puppies can cause death. Puppies with a heavy roundworm infestation have a pot-bellied appearance and a dull coat. The usual signs are vomiting, diarrhea, loss of weight, and failure to thrive. Worms may be passed in the stool.

In adult dogs, only a few larvae return to the dog's intestine. The others encyst and remain dormant in tissue. During the late stages of pregnancy, these dormant larvae are released and are carried to the unborn puppies. Larvae are also carried to puppies in breast milk. Worming the bitch before or during pregnancy does not prevent roundworm infestations since the medication does not work on encysted larvae. Consequently, many puppies are born with roundworms. Roundworms may be treated with Piperazine, Task, or Telmintic.

Hookworms are small thin worms, about one-quarter to one-half inch long, that fasten to the wall of the small intestine and draw blood from the host. The worms are contracted through larvae in contaminated soil or feces. The immature worms migrate to the intestines where they mature and pass eggs. Unborn puppies can contract hookworms while still in the uterus. Newborns ingest the larvae from the milk of an infested dam and can become ill and die rapidly. The signs of acute hookworm infestation are anemia and diarrhea with bloody stools. Acute infestations are usually seen in two to eight-week-old puppies but can occur in older dogs. Hookworms are diagnosed by microscopic examination of a stool sample. Many dogs who recover from hookworms carry cysts in their tissues that can create a new outbreak during a period of stress or illness. There are a number of wormers that can be used on hookworms, including Telmintic. However, puppies with acute hookworms need your veterinarian's care. Disophenol is an injection that your veterinarian may want to use.

Whipworms vary in length from two to three inches and resemble a small whip in appearance, but they are seldom seen by the owner. Symptoms are similar to those for hookworm except that diarrhea is not always present. In some cases the dog's bowel movement may vary from start to finish, beginning with normal stool and ending in a liquid form that is often heavily traced with blood. The adults live in the dog's caecum, an out-of-the-way organ, which makes it difficult to treat them. Heavy infestations occur where the soil is badly contaminated. Dogs with these heavy infestations lose weight, have frequent diarrhea, and are generally unthrifty. Dogs in these areas need frequent stool checks. Milibis, Dichlorvos, Telmintic, and Whipcide are all effective against whipworms.

Heartworms are now found in every part of the country, although they are more prevalent in some areas. The worm is transmitted by a mosquito feeding on an infected dog and then biting another dog. The worm starts out in the dog's blood but resides in the heart—therefore the name "heartworm." Heartworms are round in cross section and slender in diameter, and they vary from three to five inches in length. When they are present in quantity, they can impair the flow of blood. Symptoms may include shortness of breath, lack of energy, and a cough. The only way to detect heartworm is by microscopic examination of a blood sample, which should be done twice a year.

To prevent heartworm, your dog needs to be tested to be pronounced free of heartworms. The dog may then placed be on a heartworm preventative on a daily basis or on a newer pill now available that needs to be taken only once a month. If microfilariae are found in the blood the prevention *cannot* be given, as this could cause a *fatal* reaction.

A dog tested positive for heartworm can be treated and may be able to lead a normal life. In some cases the adult worms need to be surgically removed.

Coccidia is a protozoan disease (one-celled animal) that is not visible to the eye but must be diagnosed under a microscope from a fresh stool sample. Puppies acquire the infestation from infection from contaminated surroundings or from their mother if she is a carrier. Five to seven days after the ingestion, infective cysts appear in the feces. The first sign is mild diarrhea that gradually becomes mucuslike and bloody. Then there is loss of appetite, weakness, dehydration, and anemia. There can also be a cough, runny nose, and runny eyes. Coccidia can be carried in the stools of puppies without causing any problem until a stress factor such as worms or other illness reduces the dog's resistance. Dogs that have recovered can become carriers.

The infected puppies require treatment of all symptoms and administration of Amprolium, which is effective against only one stage in the life cycle of the coccidia. For this reason it must be given daily over a ten-day period. *The best prevention of coccidia is cleanliness and good sanitation.* It is especially important that all stools be removed promptly from the dog's kennel and yard area.

Demodectic mange is a disease caused by a microscopic mite, the demodex canis. Most dogs have Demodex mites living in the pores of their skin, acquired early in life and usually causing no symptoms. These mites are not completely understood but it is thought that they produce a substance that lowers the dog's natural resistance to them, thus allowing them to multiply on the dog. It has also been suggested that stress such as an infestation of roundworm also lowers the dog's natural resistance. Demodectic mange first manifests itself as a thinning of the hair around the eyes, mouth, or front legs. As it progresses, patches of hair, about an inch in diameter, are lost. In some cases demodectic mange can become generalized with numerous patches that form larger areas that sometimes form sores and crusts. Demodectic mange is diagnosed from microscopic examination of skin scrapings under the supervision of a veterinarian. Mineral oil or an ointment should be applied first to the dogs eyes, as a protection from the 4 percent Ronnel in propylene glycol that is used to treat the patches.

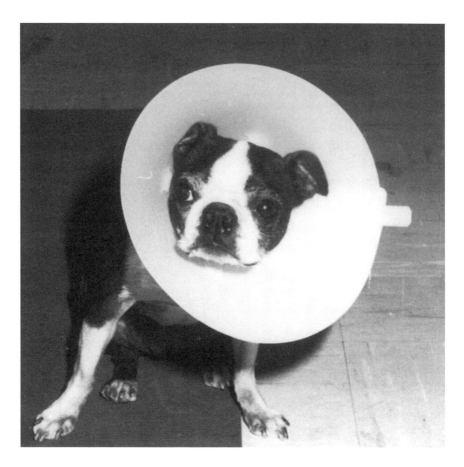

An Elizabethan collar can restrain the rear feet from scratching the head and ears or work to keep the dog from biting stitches on other parts of the body.

Scabies (sarcoptic mange) is also caused by a microscopic mite and is also diagnosed by microscopic examination of skin scrapings. These mites tunnel under the skin and cause severe itching. They lay their eggs under the skin; these eggs hatch in three to ten days. The first signs are red bumps, which are insect bites that later begin to ooze and form crusts and scabs. Hair loss is noted. In the final stage, the skin becomes thick and darkly pigmented. Sarcoptic mange is treated by bathing the dog in an insecticide dip such as lime-sulphur, ronnel, or malathion. At least three dips are given at intervals of ten days, with a fourth sometimes required. Cortisone can be given to relieve severe itching, and antibiotics are used if there are infected sores.

Although demodectic and sarcoptic mange are both caused by mites, *sarcoptic mange is highly contagious* while demodectic mange is normally noncontagious.

Conjunctivitis is an inflammation of the membrane lining the inner surface of the eyelids and the surface of the eyeball. It can be caused by foreign bodies in the eye, such as hair or dirt. There is a watery discharge. If the discharge is thick, with pus and possible crusting over the eyelids, this indicates a bacterial infection that requires a culture to identify. Mild forms can be treated at home by washing the eye with a boric acid solution. If there is bacteria present it must be treated with antibiotics.

Juvenile cataracts are one of the most serious genetic disorders in Boston Terriers. A cataract is the loss of the normal transparency of the eye lens. Any spot on the lens that is opaque, regardless of its size, technically is a cataract. The Boston Terrier Standard therefore states that "any trace of blue" in the eyes is a disqualification. Some cataracts are clearly visible to the eye, while others are diagnosed by the veterinary ophthalmologist by a CERF test. Visible cataracts can be merely flecks in the eye and can vary in color from white to milky gray to blueish white. Cataracts can also develop in diabetics and in older dogs. Most dogs eight years of age and older have some degree of haziness to the lenses. However, *even when they appear quite opaque, they still may have adequate vision.* When blindness occurs it may be corrected by cataract extraction. While this can restore vision, some visual acuity is lost, as the lens is no longer present to focus light on the retina.

This is a serious problem in Boston Terriers and it is important that carrier dogs not be bred.

Herpes Virus in puppies normally occurs between five and twenty-one days of age. It develops with no symptoms apparent until it reaches the final stage in which the puppy stops nursing, develops chills, and has abdominal distention accompanied by a yellowish green diarrhea. The pup loses coordination, and cries in agony with abdominal spasms. Nothing can relieve the condition at this point, and death usually occurs within 24 hours.

Puppies probably acquire the infection while passing through the birth canal during whelping. It can also be spread to the litter by someone who has handled an infected dog. As there is no vaccine available, the only treatment is to raise infected puppies in an incubator that maintains a temperature of 100 degrees, as the virus does not survive at temperatures above 98 degrees. Autopsies performed on puppies who died of Herpes Virus show red spots on the kidneys. Puppies who have survived Herpes Virus in an incubator frequently succumb to kidney failure at eight to ten months of age.

A **swimmer** is a flat-chested puppy that lies with its legs sticking out to the side like a turtle, instead of under it. This condition is due to a weakness of the muscles that pull the legs into the body. This condition usually occurs in an overweight puppy. It is important, to see that the puppies are kept on a non-slippery surface when they are first learning to stand and walk. The puppy should be encouraged to sleep on its side, as the flat chest is caused from sleeping on the stomach. This can be accomplished by placing a hobble (tie) made from tape on the puppy's front legs to keep the puppy from sleeping on its stomach. This also helps to keep the legs under the pup when it tries to stand. The tape should be positioned from elbow to elbow. You will also need to work several times a day to help the puppy stand and make a complete recovery.

Puppies can develop two types of **hernias,** those that can be pushed back into the abdomen through the abdominal wall and those that cannot. If the hernia can be pushed back through the abdominal wall, it may close on its own as the puppy grows. It must be watched to see if it will close; if not, it will need to be repaired. If it cannot be pushed back, the hernia requires repair by a veterinarian. Your veterinarian will be able to advise you when surgery is required. The two areas in which the hernias appear are the groin, known as inguinal hernias, and the naval, known as umbilical hernias.

The final health problem for many Boston Terriers is **old age**. Both behavioral and physical changes occur. Older dogs are less energetic and tend to sleep a lot. They are less tolerant of change in their routine.

While exercise is beneficial, the older dog should not be exercised beyond the normal limit of activity. The dog may also need to be covered at night and may *lose some hearing and some sight. Urinary tract problems* may develop, and the dog may have trouble controlling urine. If your dog has loose teeth, have them removed. *Tooth and gum problems* are common in older dogs and can interfere with eating unless properly treated. This is only one reason why *diet* is of the utmost importance in caring for the older dog. Not only will your dog need a diet of lower fat and calories but it may also require a special prescription diet—such as K/D for a Boston that has reduced kidney function.

You will need to have your older Boston Terrier checked regularly by the veterinarian and lab work done to determine any diseases or conditions that may be present. Aging Bostons may acquire heart disease or cancer. Consult your veterinarian about caring for these illnesses. It is important to remember that when the dog is in pain and is suffering with no hope of recovery, this is the time to make the final decision in order to relieve your dog's suffering by requesting euthanasia. This is done humanely by the veterinarian.

EMERGENCY FIRST AID

CPR or **cardiopulmonary resuscitation** is a combination of artificial respiration and heart massage. Heart massage by itself provides movement of air as well as pumping of blood, but it works best when combined with mouth-to-nose breathing. There are two methods of artificial respiration—chest compression, which is the easiest to perform, and mouth-to-nose forced breathing, which is used when the chest is punctured or chest compression is ineffective.

To administer chest compressions you begin by checking the mouth for any foreign objects and removing them. You then lay the dog on a hard flat surface with the *right side down*. Place both hands on the chest, press down firmly, and release quickly. *You should be able to hear air moving in and out as you do the compressions*. If you do not, you need to begin mouth-to-nose resuscitation. If you do hear air moving, continue until the dog is breathing independently.

To perform mouth-to-nose resuscitation, check the mouth for foreign objects, pull the tongue forward, and close the mouth, sealing the lips with your hand. Then place your mouth over the dog's nose and blow into it steadily for three seconds. This will expand the chest. Then remove your mouth from the dog's nose to let the air come back out. Continue until the dog is breathing independently.

If the dog does not have a heartbeat (pulse) you will need to perform heart massage. Lay the dog on the right side, placing your thumb on one side of the sternum and your fingers on the *other side* right behind the elbows. Compress the chest firmly six times, wait five seconds for the chest to expand, then repeat until the heart is beating on its own or until no heart beat has been felt for five minutes.

If the dog has a **foreign object** lodged in the larynx, you must go to a veterinarian immediately. If the dog collapses from lack of air, however, you won't have time to go to the vet and so you must perform the **Heimlich maneuver** immediately. First lay the dog on the side, placing your palms just behind the last rib, and give four quick thrusts. This usually dislodges the object by producing a forceful exhalation of air. Check the mouth to see if the object has been dislodged; if not, repeat the four quick thrusts.

Burns are treated according to the degree of damage. *Superficial burns* are treated by applying cold water soaks or ice packs for thirty minutes to relieve the pain. Gently wash the area with an antibacterial soap, apply a topical antibiotic ointment, and protect the area by covering with a loose fitting gauze dressing. *Chemical burns* need to be flushed with large amounts of water. *Acid burns* are neutralized by rinsing with a solution of four tablespoons of baking soda in a pint of water, and alkalia is neutralized by rinsing with a solution of two tablespoons of vinegar to a pint of water. Then blot dry, apply antibiotic ointment, and bandage loosely. Deep burns need to be treated immediately by a veterinarian, although if a large area of the dog is involved fluid seeping from burns can lead to shock.

Dehydration is a condition caused by excessive loss of body fluids due to fever, vomiting, or diarrhea. Early signs of dehydration are dryness of the mouth and loss of elasticity of the skin; later signs are sunken eyeballs and circulatory collapse. In the early stage, if the dog is not vomiting an electrolyte solution such as Pedialyte may be given orally. It is best to seek veterinarian treatment to have fluids intravenously administered if the dog is noticeably dehydrated.

Boston Terriers are highly susceptible to **overheating** due to the dark coat, which holds and intensifies the heat, and to the fact that they are a brachycephalic (short-muzzled) breed. Dogs pant to exchange warm air for cool air, which is not an efficient process in extreme heat. For that reason, *never leave a Boston in a car in warm weather* or in the sun without plenty of shade and water, and do not allow it too much strenuous exercise during the heat of the day. If the condition is in its early stages, the dog can usually be quickly cooled down in air conditioning. For a dog that is seriously overheated you can either immerse it in a tub of cool water or hose it down with a garden hose. A dog with heatstroke may have swelling of the throat and may require a shot of cortisone from the veterinarian.

Poisons are from many sources, including plants, petroleum, and medications. The first thing is to identify the poison. Read the label (if relevant) and then *call your local Poison Control Center* for specific instructions. You should induce vomiting *unless* the dog has swallowed a petroleum product, acid, alkali, solvent, or strong cleaner. If the dog is unconscious, or if more than two hours have elapsed since the poison was ingested, vomiting should *not* be induced. Vomiting can best be induced by administering one teaspoon of Syrup of Ipecac for each ten pounds of the dog's weight. You should prevent absorption of the poison into the intestinal tract by administering a solution of one gram activated charcoal to 4 cc water. Administer one teaspoonful per each two pounds of the dog's weight. Half an hour later, administer one teaspoonful of Milk of Magnesia for each five pounds of the dogs weight. As soon as you have the dog stabilized, take both the dog and the poison in its original container to the veterinarian.

Wounds are usually caused either by laceration or puncture (bites). Either type of wound should first be cleaned to remove all dirt and contamination to reduce the risk of infection. Wash your hands and be sure to use sterile instruments and dressings. Cleanse the wound with hydrogen peroxide and rinse with water. Then apply an antibiotic ointment and bandage. Any wounds over half an inch in length will probably need to be sutured by your veterinarian to facilitate healing and to prevent infection and scarring.

Ch. O.J.'s First Class Fortune Cooky is a Best in Show winner, bred by Ola Jeanne McCollough and owned by Joanne Hearst.

CHAPTER

12

Conformation

The Making of a Champion

THIS IS ONE OF THE FUN PARTS OF BREEDING BOSTON TERRIERS. THIS IS WHERE you get to take that beautiful new puppy you either just bought or bred and raised yourself and really show it off. As breeders and exhibitors, we are always looking for that extra-special show dog, who not only is an exemplary representative of the Standard, but who also loves to show. The love of shows is something you have to cultivate in the dog yourself, through the time you put into training. Some show attitude may be genetic, but the rest is up to you.

Most Boston Terriers will never see the show ring. They and their owners are perfectly happy at home. There are no doubt many beautiful Boston Terriers happily fulfilling their lives as pets and enjoying just being a part of a family. Other beautiful show dogs look forward to dog shows and to getting in the ring and doing their thing. These dogs enjoy being a part of the family too and also enjoy a good relationship with their handler if he or she is not the owner. If you are not sure if your Boston Terrier is show quality you can attend some shows to see how the dogs that are being shown compare to your dog.

TO BEGIN

At this time we will assume that you have either bought or bred a beautiful, sound Boston Terrier puppy and you have great hopes of finishing a championship or even dreams of "Specialing." Only time will tell. If you see no apparent faults, now is the time to begin training. You will need to reevaluate constantly as your dog develops before you begin to put time, effort, and money into exhibiting. Yes, showing dogs can be an expensive hobby. You must pay entry fees, which are the smallest part of the expense. The larger expenses come with traveling in every direction to show your dog; sometimes you travel hundreds of miles in search of that last elusive major or to attend a Specialty show. Many times you arrive at the show only to find that the major has been broken or that the judge that you were absolutely sure would like your dog prefers another specimen.

Most people go to dog shows to win, and they make sure they have a dog with a reasonable chance of winning. With this in mind, you need to make sure that your Boston Terrier is a reasonably good specimen of the breed. Your dog need not be perfect. *None* out there is perfect. **The perfect Boston Terrier has not yet been bred.** This is the goal that keeps breeders constantly trying to improve their breeding. Your Boston must meet the basic requirements of structure, soundness, type, and balance as outlined in the Standard, and should move with determination and style. We won't say that without every one of these requirements your dog won't ever win, but we will say that without them the dog won't win very often.

TRAINING

Training is best started by getting the puppy used to wearing a collar for several days before you attempt to attach a lead. The first several times that you put a lead on, you may want to let your puppy go where it wants to as it gets used to the feel of someone on the other end of the lead. After your dog becomes used to the feel of the lead, you will want to try to get the puppy to walk alongside of you. More than likely your pup will have new ideas on which way to go. At this point, you need lots of patience with your Boston puppy and lots of repetition. Do *not* try to train a puppy for too long a period of time. It is better to go out more often and for short periods of time. Reward your dog with praise and a small treat. You don't want to jerk the puppy so that it learns to dislike the lead, as you will want your Boston to walk proudly and to enjoy being on a lead.

Two other very important things to teach the show puppy at an early age are to stand on a grooming table while being examined and to pose "stacked" on the ground. Both of these tasks should be taught as fun things to do and they should be rewarded when done well. Boston Terriers are lively, intelligent dogs. They will try hard to please their owners and appreciate a pat on the head and a few words of praise and a special treat.

Lead Work

You will want to begin training in a quiet area with as few distractions as possible so that your puppy will be able to pay attention to you. Once a dog has learned the basics of both gaiting on a lead and posing stacked on the ground, you are ready to go to an area full of distractions such as a shopping mall or a neighborhood street. You now need to have your puppy gait and pose stacked amid busy surroundings. This will teach your dog to focus on you instead of on the distractions from the surroundings.

Teach your Boston Terrier puppy to move beside you on a loose lead. Do not use a tight lead as this tends to make the puppy look "strung up" and does not give a favorable impression of the dog's movement.

Stacking

After your Boston puppy is walking confidently on a lead, you will want to concentrate on stacking. Start with posing the head, then placing the feet, then posing the head again. Put the lead in your right hand and place your left hand on the dog's loin for steadying. If you are fortunate enough to have a near perfect dog, this could be the extent of your stacking.

If you do not have the perfect Boston Terrier or the perfectly trained Boston Terrier puppy, you will need to do quite a bit more. Keep in mind that a puppy has a short attention span, so gradually increase the length

Ch. Barra's Highland Lassie, bred and owned by Elizabeth McNeil of Maryland, was handled by Jodi Ghaster.

Ch. M L's Cookie Monster, bred and owned by Mary Lou Zimmerman Dreher and owned by Michele DeJulia of New Jersey.

of time that you ask the puppy to stand still in each session. Remember not to overdo the training session, and continue to praise the puppy and reward with a treat when you are finished.

Slip the collar up under the puppy's chin, making sure that any loose skin is below the collar on the side of the head. Set up the front feet. To do this, grasp the foreleg at the *elbow* and place the foot so that the pastern and elbow are in a straight line with the highest point of withers. Feet should point straight ahead. At the same time, turn the dog's head in the opposite direction from the leg that you are adjusting. This shifts the dog's weight to the other legs and makes the leg you are placing easier to move. Place the right foreleg with your right hand and the left foreleg with your left hand. Your thumb should always be in front of the elbow.

To set up the hindquarters, grasp the hock joint and place the foot so that the rear pasterns are perpendicular to the ground with toes pointing forward. Use your left hand to place both rear feet with your thumb at the top of the hock. When placing the feet, always remember to lift them rather than sliding them into place. When you have finished setting your Boston Terrier, the dog should appear square.

Do not hover over your Boston puppy when stacking. When setting up on the table, step back after setting the dog up. If you are setting up on the floor, get down on both knees and sit back on your heels.

FIRST MATCH

At this point, one of the best things to do to get your Boston Terrier puppy ready for that first match is to go to a training class if you have one available in your area. This will not only get the dog used to being in a ring with other dogs, but it will also give it the experience of having a stranger doing an examination on a table, as a judge would.

When you are asked to move individually, you may want to do a courtesy half circle in front of the judge, moving clockwise. If you are showing a dog with a poor front, eliminate the courtesy circle and proceed down the mat. When gaiting around the ring, keep your eyes on your dog, the judge, the dog in front of you, and the mat. Don't worry—soon you *will* be able to do all of that at the same time.

The training class will also get your puppy accustomed to the other dogs and handlers being in the ring. Do not let your puppy play with, jump on, or sniff the dogs in front or behind it when another handler is trying to gait or stack the dog. When you move, your puppy should gait in the center of the mat. When moving straight down and back towards the judge, slowdown the puppy as you approach the judge and stop in front to bait your puppy. The distance you stop from the judge should depend on your dog's front. If your puppy has a good front, give the judge ample room to see it. If your puppy's front is not ideal, bring your puppy close up so the judge is looking down on the puppy.

GROOMING

We are indeed fortunate that the Boston Terrier as a breed requires only a minimum of grooming as compared to some of the coated breeds. The Boston Terrier should be kept clean at all times, regardless of whether the dog is being shown. Nails should be kept trimmed at all times to keep a dog up on its toes and to keep the dog's pasterns from weakening.

If you intend to show, your puppy will need to get used to being groomed. Grooming should begin with a bath. The dog should then be placed on a grooming table daily and brushed. Brushing is good for the skin and coat, and it will get your dog looking forward to being on the grooming table, being groomed, and getting some extra attention.

You should also begin nail trimming on a regular basis at an early age. This can be accomplished by using either a clipper or a nail grinder. When trimming nails, be particularly careful not to cut into the quick, the inner portion of the nail, which on white nails appears pink. If you use a clipper, you should follow up with a file to smooth off any rough edges.

Before showing, you may want to do a little extra grooming, such as removing whiskers, trimming the hair on the neck (collar), and clipping hair between the toes and any other wild hair that keeps your Boston puppy from having a clean, smooth look.

Another grooming procedure that can be done a few days before the show is to thin the hair on the dog's neck, by using a hair shaper, for a smoother, finer look. This is done by pulling the shaper down the neck following the direction in which the hair grows to remove a small amount of the hair. You must be careful not to remove too much hair in any one spot because this can leave a thin spot that would detract from the dog's appearance. The purpose of this procedure is to accentuate the continu-

Ch. Maximillian's Mon Petit, bred by Barbara and Edward Lohringel and owned by Joanne Hearst and Ann McCammon.

ous flow. The neck, cheeks, and ears should all blend. It is best to practice this procedure far in advance of any shows, as it will take you a while to get the feel of it and you are sure to leave some uneven spots the first time or two. You need to allow ample time for the dog's hair to grow back where you have created a nick with the hair shaper. If you know someone who can demonstrate this procedure, all grooming on the Boston Terrier, so much the better.

THE SHOW

Showing dogs is a sport, and all participants need to exhibit good sportsmanship. If you lose at one show, it does not make the dog any less valuable. If you win, that does not make your dog any better than before. Good dogs can sometimes lose to lesser dogs because the good ones are not in the best condition, are not well groomed, or are not properly handled, all of which are essential to winning. In addition, your dog may not be showing well on that particular day.

Every exhibitor will have to decide whether to show the dog as an owner/handler or to engage the service of a professional handler to show the dog. The Boston Terrier is a breed in which many owners enjoy the satisfaction of exhibiting their own dogs. They are many other owners, however, who prefer to have their dogs shown by handlers. Among the reasons for this are the fact that an experienced handler can present a Boston to the utmost potential. The professional attends shows every weekend; the owner, however, may not have the time. Although employing a good handler is not cheap, it is far more expensive and time consuming for an inexperienced handler to show a dog. Then again, you may like learning the skills of showing your own dog in this competitive sport.

When you are going to a show, it is best not to feed your dog before traveling in the car. Boston puppies are more alert and show better on an empty stomach, and they really don't get car sick if they haven't eaten recently.

Get to the match ahead of time so that your puppy has time to adjust to the surroundings. Also, be sure to take your pup to the exercise area before going into the ring. Keep your mind and your eyes on your dog and on the judge during the entire time you are in the ring. Use some

(left to right) Ch. Al-Mar's Armed & Dangerous, Ch. Al-Mar's By Invitation Only, and Ch. Al-Mar's Formal Attire, bred and owned by Patrice and Susan Kennedy of Arizona.

bait or a squeak toy to keep your Boston alert. If your dog gets out of step when you gait, stop and start over again.

Spending too much time trying to conceal a fault may draw attention to it. Also, don't position your dog so as to hide another dog from the judge's view, and pay attention to what is going on in the ring. You should be aware of what pattern the judge is going to ask you to do, and you should know when to move up and which dog started so that when the last dog is moved you are getting your dog set up for the final examination.

Remember that if you do not place in the ribbons this time there is always another match or another show. You are simply getting one particular judge's opinion on that particular day. Congratulate the winner. If you are the winner, be sure to say something nice to the handler who has just lost to you. Remember to be confident and enjoy yourself.

PHOTOGRAPHS

If you had a good day and won, you will want to get a picture of your dog with the judge. Remember that a picture is worth a thousand words. Check with the ring steward to find out when pictures will be taken. When the judge and photographer are ready, set your dog up on the grooming table and stacked in front of you making sure the topline is level and all four feet are squarely in place. The photographer will throw a toy or some object to get the dog to animate at the right time. You may want to practice taking some snapshots at home and getting the dog used to posing for photographs.

Remember that a Boston Terrier will show up better in the picture if *you* wear bright or light-colored clothing. Do not have your hands on the dog in the picture. Have several pictures taken in order to choose the best one.

No matter how big a win you have, never publish a picture that does not show your dog to best advantage. If you do, those who have never seen the dog in person will remember the poor specimen they saw in the photo.

Good luck and have fun!

OTCH Brother Mac Duff completed an Obedience Trial Championship after being both the Highest Scoring Dog in Trial as well as earning the Highest Combined score in Open and Utility that day. This was a great triumph and an indication that Mac Duff is indeed a winner for owner Ellen Dresselhuis.

CHAPTER

$$\boxed{13}$$

Obedience

Second Nature to the Boston Terrier

by Alicia Parry

OBEDIENCE STARTED TO BECOME POPULAR WITH BOSTON TERRIER OWNERS AT the end of the 1980s and in the early 1990s. The Boston Terrier Club of America sponsored their first Obedience Trial in 1989; a number of local Boston Terrier Specialty Clubs are now sanctioned by the American Kennel Club to hold Trials, with even more clubs working on qualifying matches. More breeders are training a favorite and are competing. In addition, dogs who are unable to go in the conformation ring for disqualifications such as missing ears and surgical scars, and all those sold whether as pets or as show dogs can be fine partners in Obedience. In fact, rescue dogs with ILP numbers (indefinite listing privileges) can compete and receive high scores. In 1992, The Boston Terrier Club of America honored the breed's first Obedience Trial Champion (OTCH), Brother Mac Duff, and his partner, Ellen Dresselhuis.

Ch. Karadin Fulla Fun, C.D., bred by Ethel Braunstein and owned by Laurel B. Tierney, proved that a Group winner can also be an Obedience title holder.

Ch. Ace and Angel's King Tuff, Am. CDX/Can. C.D., owned by Margaret Staley of Wisconsin.

OTCH Brother Mac Duff takes a jump that he always managed to clear by at least a foot!

Boston Terriers make good Obedience candidates because of their lively enthusiasm, desire to please, and general intelligence. They need a gentle, if firm, approach, and they respond positively to handler praise, enthusiasm for their efforts, and often a tidbit reward.

This chapter is not intended to teach you the skill and precision needed for high scores or titles, but rather is intended as an overview.

WHY OBEDIENCE?

Why should you consider Obedience training? Because it is a sport, a fun activity with other dog people or club members, and *mainly because it is fun for your Boston Terrier*. Obedience training builds a bond between Boston and handler, creating a real partnership.

Obedience also develops some very important controls for the safety of Boston Terriers and all dogs. Obedience increases the self confidence of the Boston Terrier, and so it can be used effectively with a reluctant conformation ring candidate. Obedience challenges the Boston Terrier, who responds with efforts to learn and to succeed. As more Boston Terriers appear in the Obedience ring, spectators take an additional view of the Boston's abilities. Then, when breeders know something about the sport from personal experience, they are in a much better position to discuss Obedience with new puppy owners. A final thought: Boston puppies going to an Obedience home are normally there for life. You know that your Boston puppy will have a loving home and good care if an Obedience enthusiast buys it.

The three most-titled Obedience Boston Terriers, all owned by Trophy Fredrick of Pennsylvania. In front is Trophy's Incredible Cricket, Am U.D., Bda U.D., Can U.D. On the left is Warder's Fascinating Frolic Am. U.D., Can. U.D., and Bda C.D., and on the right is Mister Warder's Mighty Mouse, Am C.D.X., and Can. C.D.X.

THE TITLES

	Companion Dog	Companion Dog Excellent	Utility Dog
	Novice (C.D.)	*Open (C.D.X.)*	*Utility (U.D.)*
Heeling	1. Walk at Heel; Neck under handler's left hip. Change pace. Change direction. On lead. 2. Same pattern Off Lead. 3. Sit automatically when handler stops. 4. Heel a figure 8 with 2 halts on a lead.	1 2 4 Off-lead	**Signal Exercise:** Heel pattern using hand signals. No voice. Then halt standing. On signal, down with handler 40' away. Sit, Come, Finish on signal only.
Finish	Return to handler's left side & sit. Ends most exercises.		
Stand for Examination	Stand without moving with handler 6 feet away & allow exam by stranger—touched 3 places.	None	Walk 6 feet with handler, stop short on command as handler goes 6 feet more. A Show exam minus mouth. On command, return to Heel by handler.

	Novice	*Open*	*Utility*
Recall	Wait for command. Come directly to handler. Finish.	Same, but add a Drop as the dog comes to the handler.	See Signal Exercise.
Sit-Stay	Stay 1 minute. Handler across ring.	Stay 3 minutes. Handler out of sight.	None
Down-Stay	Stay 3 minutes. Handler across the ring.	Stay 5 minutes. Handler out of sight.	See Signal Exercise.
Retrieve On the Flat	None	Go out, get wooden dumbbell. Return directly & sit. Hand dumbbell over when commanded.	None
Retrieve Over High Jump	None	Dumbbell is tossed over high jump. Dog jumps high jump, retrieves dumb-bell, returns over jump, hands over dumbbell on command.	None
Directed Retrieve (Retrieve Gloves)	None	None	3 white gloves set 15 feet apart, 20 feet from dog. Judge names glove. Handler uses voice & arm

	Novice	Open	Utility
			signal. Dog gets directed glove & hands over glove to handler when told.
Scent Discrimination Exercise	None	None	4 metal, 4 leather articles set out. Pile mixed up & articles are placed 20 feet from dog and approximately 6 inches apart from each other. Dog must retrieve one metal article and one leather article (placed by judge) which the handler scents, using only hands. It is placed among the others being dropped off a clip board, each article separately.
Jumping	None	1–See Retrieving Over High Jump 2–Dog sits 8 feet or more from Broad Jump. Jumps on command, comes to front. Finishes.	Directed Jumping. On command dog leaves handler's side, goes straight out until called & told to sit, when dog turns

Novice	Open	Utility
		to face handler and sits. There are 2 jumps 18 to 20 feet apart. 1 a High Jump, 1 a Bar Jump. Handler commands & signals dog to jump. When back at Heel, dog is sent out again & is commanded to take the other jump.

The chart shows the basic work required for each of the three American Kennel Club Obedience titles. To get the OTCH (Obedience Trial Championship) title, a Utility Dog (U.D.) must place in Open B and Utility classes. The Novice work sets the basis for the advanced work, with five of the six exercises teaching handler control and self-control. To get a title, the partnership must earn more than 50 of the score for each exercise, plus a minimum total score of 170 out of a possible 200 points. The same rule applies to all titles.

Practical Applications

Looking again at the chart, three of the exercises stand out for their *safety features*. Long Sit and Long Downs, particularly out of sight, mean control in an emergency.

The Drop on Recall, an Open exercise often started as Drop on command, can prevent a moving animal from entering a life-threatening situation. Taught correctly, the Drop prevents returning to the handler, which could also lead the dog into a life-threatening situation. It can be more useful than "Come." The Recall is a vital exercise that is absolutely necessary, but a fast-moving dog leaving a scene will not respond to "Come" as fast as "Down." All these exercises should be taught with *both* voice and hand commands.

You appreciate the dog Heeling beside you, but the Boston, on the other hand, probably prefers jumping, retrieving, and the challenge of scent work!

OBEDIENCE IS NOT YANK, PULL, AND YELL. The lead is a reminder and should *never* be used as punishment. Show your Boston Terrier what you want, and at the same time, use the command word. The activity should be *fun* for your dog. Satisfying experience for both you and your dog. This is a partnership. You need each other to succeed, and trust is of the essence. Some Bostons need a daily session. Other Bostons seem to benefit from time off. Knowing the learning style of your four-footed partner makes your life much happier.

TRAINING IN OBEDIENCE

Every year at the Boston Terrier National Specialty Obedience Trial, there is someone who comes and shows who has never seen another Boston in Obedience and who has never had the chance to train at a club. This can be done because there are a lot of good books available that teach how to train and that give specific techniques for all parts of the exercises. Before buying, however, get some advice. It is very important to know which books not to use and which books are weak. The training of police, army, and narcotics dogs is done quite differently than the training of our sensitive, loving Boston Terriers. To get advice, order books on interlibrary loan from your local library. Contact the American Kennel Club Obedience Department or ask the Boston Terrier Club of America Obedience Chairperson. All these people can advise you. There are all kinds of Obedience books out there, so be sure that you get a good one for Boston Terriers.

Novice Stand for Examination. *Off lead, the handler stands six feet in front of the dog. The dog may be allowed to sniff before the judge touches only the top of the dog's head, the withers, and the back near the tail. This is also good experience for the conformation ring.*

Stay hand signal. *The hand goes in front of the dog's nose but* does not touch *the dog.*

Upon hearing the verbal signal, given simultaneously with the hand signal, Ch. Isolda C.D.X. virtually explodes out of the Sit position to retrieve Glove #2.

Nice clean pick up. This dog likes to circle part way around before actually retrieving.

She returns to sit directly in front and holds the glove until the judge gives the command to give the glove to the handler.

Ch. Isolda C.D.X., My Jaunty Ensign, Ch. Charger's Duchess, and Coquette II, C.D., all owned by Alicia Parry and all Obedience trained.

The dog must be taught to take an object on command everytime. A dumbbell is not a toy, and this not a game.

After learning to take the dumbbell on command, the dog must learn to stand and reach for it at eye level. The handler is Alicia H. Parry.

With your dog on lead, start with placing the dumbbell on the floor (shown), then toss it, gradually increasing the distance. Each time your dog retrieves the dumbbell, call him back; he may be given a small pop with the lead to bring him directly back.

Dog returning with the dumbbell after retrieving it.

This Boston is choosing the one metal article scented by the handler.

She confidently returns with the correct one.

The dog must sit in front of the handler and give the article to the handler on command. This handler's choice of shoes, which catch the dog's peripheral vision, can be a help in heeling and positioning.

Training with others is very helpful. Local classes may be available. Check to see if the trainers have trained small dogs and if there will be some in the class. If there are no local classes, try Obedience magazines such as *Front and Finish* and *Off Lead*. The former will have advertisements of training seminars and clinics. You can spend a fortune on puppy classes, which we do not recommend, but a good beginners' class from a local club or individual trainer will get you and your Boston off to a good start.

If you like the idea of training, it is now time to get detailed advice from a trainer, club, seminar, or book. Start making plans for a match or two and get ready for the shows. Obedience people are great people who are more than willing to share tips, help you with problems, and get you and your Boston ready to form a successful partnership and a deeper bond.

C H A P T E R

14

One of the Family

Living and Traveling
with the Boston Terrier

FOR OVER A HUNDRED YEARS THE BOSTON TERRIER HAS BEEN AN IDEAL COMPANION. The Boston Terrier is equally at home on a country estate or in a small city apartment. This breed does not have to be able to hunt, herd, or retrieve, as all any Boston Terrier owner needs is a friendly companion. And how the Boston Terrier fills this description with alertness, intelligence, and friendliness. This truly is an American original, with the jaunty movement of a compact body, the dapper markings on a beautiful square head, and the intelligence conveyed in those expressive eyes.

The Boston Terrier is an extremely easy dog to live with, wanting only to please. This makes Bostons extremely easy to train. Bostons are strictly house dogs, they are not able to cope with the extreme cold of winter, being a short-coated dog. Nor can they deal with extreme heat, as the dark coat absorbs heat and the extremely short muzzle with a slightly elongated palate can cause overheating quite easily.

Ch. Karadin Our Mariah, bred by Ethel Braunstein and owned by Ethel Braunstein and Ron Clark.

Your Boston needs to be loved and properly cared for, with its required food on a regular schedule. It is also most important that all inoculations be kept up to date and that you have stool samples checked regularly.

Boston Terriers are willing learners, but you need to let them know from the beginning the rules of your house and what they can and cannot do. Most Bostons seem to have favorite places in the house, such as a place where they can lie in a sunny spot, a nice warm spot next to the fireplace or radiator or their favorite spot of all—snuggled next to you. Boston Terriers are excellent dogs with children, but small children need to be told how to treat the Boston in order to ensure the safety and well-being of a Boston puppy or a new adult. Remember that this is a small dog. In addition, make sure that your Boston Terrier is not allowed to roam the neighborhood, as we have heard many tragic stories from owners who thought that they had their dogs "trained to stay" in their own yards. It takes only a female in season (if your dog is male), a cat, or a rabbit to lure a Boston from the yard. An exercise pen could substitute for a fenced yard. Even if your neighbors like your dog, they will not long appreciate any dog roaming loose in *their* yard. Most areas now have leash laws that prohibit owners from allowing their dogs to run loose. Most Boston Terriers look forward to a walk on a leash with their owner as the highlight of the day.

VACATIONS

When your family goes on vacation, you must make the decision as to whether or not your Boston Terrier goes with you. Many motels do allow pets, but you need to consider what you plan to do on the trip. If you will be spending most of your day not at the motel but visiting museums or amusement parks where dogs are not permitted, your Boston may be better off at a reputable boarding kennel back home. Be sure to inspect the facilities of the boarding kennel in advance of your trip. There are also petsitting services that allow your dog to stay comfortably at home. You may also be fortunate enough to have a friend, neighbor, or relative who is willing to care for your Boston while you are gone.

But if you are going on a vacation where you will be spending your time hiking, camping, or visiting relatives, and if you are sure that your

Tuffy and Joey, owned by Margaret Staley, are great companions for each other and their owner.

Early morning walk on the beach.

Boston is welcome, taking your dog along may be fine for all concerned. Be sure to remember that there will be times when you will go to places such as swimming pools and restaurants where dogs are not allowed. You must make provisions for a safe place where your dog will not become overheated. A car is no place *ever* to leave a Boston in warm weather as the temperature inside the car rises very quickly and a dog with a short muzzle such as a Boston will not live long. What may look like a nice shady spot to park a car could be in full sun in a short time. If you must leave your Boston in the car, the car must be in the shade with the windows open a few inches for ventilation; you should do this for no more than a few minutes.

If you do take your Boston on a trip, you will need a crate to keep your dog in for safety and to act as a seat belt. Many motels are more likely to accept dogs that are kept in crates. Never leave your dog loose and unattended in a motel room. Be sure before you leave a dog alone, even crated, that other guests will not be annoyed by continuous barking.

When staying at a motel, look for a spot away from shrubbery and flowers to exercise your dog and be sure to clean up afterward. Remember that if dog owners do not see to it that they leave the motel rooms and grounds as they found them, without soiling or damaging them, dogs will no longer be welcome in motels.

Your Boston can also travel with you by airplane. You must have an airline-approved kennel with a water dish attached inside. Some airlines still permit owners to carry on small crates as long as they fit under the seat. This works well with a Boston Terrier. This privilege may be allowed for only one dog per plane, so you need to make your arrangements well in advance. You are also required to go to your vet no more than ten days before the trip for a health certificate. Airlines reserve the right not to accept any live animals for shipment in very hot or cold weather.

Things to Do and Bring

You should be sure that your dog is wearing a collar with an identification tag. You may want to bring several bottles of water from home to eliminate the possibility of your Boston getting diarrhea from a change of water. Be sure to pack food, dishes, lead, any necessary medication, and a favorite toy. If you are interested in exhibiting your Boston, and you are traveling, to a dog show, you will need to pack grooming supplies, grooming table, and bait.

Ch. Brandy's Million Dollar Baby, bred by Bruce and Sandy Crook and owned by Ethel Braunstein.

An incomparable companion.

You will find that most Boston Terriers like nothing better than to get in the car and go. It seems as though they know they make excellent traveling companions.

THE OLDER DOG

The day will come when your Boston Terrier has gone from puppyhood to adulthood and eventually reaches old age. Older dogs are more set in their ways and usually do not adapt as well to change. They still need exercise, but not as much. They sleep more now, and they will thrive best on food that contains a lower percentage of protein and calories that is especially formulated for older dogs. As with humans, a dog is healthiest when proper weight is maintained. Your veterinarian can prescribe KD or whatever special diet may be required if your older dog has health problems. Older dogs acquire many of the same afflictions as older people, such as cataracts, deafness, kidney problems, heart problems, and cancer. Conditions such as blindness and deafness require a little more attention, and help on your part will make sure your Boston Terrier is comfortable.

When the time comes when your old dog is suffering and there is no hope of recovery, the most caring thing to do is to let your veterinarian perform euthanasia so that your friend will suffer no more.

Ch. Sovereign's Princess Sugar (lived to 18 years), Ch. Gimp's Carry on Sugar's Image (lived to 16 years), and Ch. Gimp's Bonita Koo Koo (lived to 16 years), all owned by Frank Guemple of Indiana.

CHAPTER

15

Genetic Testing in Dogs

by Kathryn T. Graves, Ph.D.

RECENT DEVELOPMENTS IN DNA TECHNOLOGY HAVE OPENED THE DOOR TO exciting possibilities for genetic testing in dogs. Two primary uses for DNA-based testing include parentage verification and identification of genetic markers for trait selection.

PARENTAGE VERIFICATION

There are several instances in which the owner of a puppy might want to verify the parentage of the dog. Maybe another stud accidentally bred the bitch after she had been bred by a different stud, and the breeder needs to know which stud sired the puppies. Someone may return a dog to a breeder, but the breeder questions that it is the same dog that he or she sold as a puppy years ago. A DNA-based test could provide a reliable means of identifying individual dogs and confirming parentage.

TRAIT TESTING

Multitudes of genetic defects exist in dogs. This is simply the result of years of *necessary inbreeding in order to establish the various breeds*. It is inevitable that, while selecting for desirable traits, certain deleterious genes that are also present in mixed breeds were retained in the population. In order to control the incidence of these problems, responsible breeders of purebred dogs must maintain strict culling programs. Even with culling and careful breeding, breeders can still find themselves frustrated by recessive traits that "pop up out of nowhere." Technology is becoming available that will allow breeders to have their stock tested for the presence of deleterious or desired genes when the dog is still a puppy, thereby saving the time and expense of showing and promoting dogs that carry serious genetic defects. The opposite is also true—more money and time can be invested in dogs with genes for desirable traits.

PARENTAGE TESTING

In order for a genetic trait to be useful in parentage testing it needs to be polymorphic—that is, there must be enough different forms of the gene to make individuals distinguishable. Unlike many other species, the dog has relatively little diversity or polymorphism in its blood groups. For example, the human ABO blood group system has three types of genes, A, B, or O. Since everyone inherits one gene from each parent, people have only one or two of these red cell factors. Even with three different factors, having blood types match does not prove parentage; it can only disprove it.

Imagine if there were only one blood type, as is the case with most of the dog's blood group systems of most dogs. *Since all dogs have the same factor, there is no way to prove or disprove parentage based on blood type.* What this means is that many dogs can have the same "blood type" even though they are unrelated. This makes it difficult, if not impossible, to determine the parentage of a puppy based on blood type alone.

Several groups have investigated the use of markers other than red cell antigens for use in determining parentage. These markers generally are blood proteins that are present in the dog's serum. Although as many as thirteen red cell antigens in eleven genetic systems have been identified in the dog (Colling and Saison, 1980), these have not proved to be sufficiently polymorphic to be useful in the identification of individuals. Blood cell enzymes have also been of limited use in parentage verification. (Juneja et al, 1987).

Several plasma proteins have been described that have increased the chances of correctly identifying the sire of a litter of puppies, but in general relying on red cell antigens and blood proteins to determine parentage in dogs has been disappointing. This is why DNA testing has been applied to parentage testing in dogs.

DNA fingerprinting is a term that has become familiar to the public, as this form of testing has been accepted as evidence in criminal trials. This technology is based on the presence of repetitive sequences in the DNA molecule. The size of these repetitive areas is apparently quite polymorphic in the dog, and so far this test is the one used to verify parentage (Jeffries and Morton, 1987). It is quite useful with regard to parentage testing, as long as samples from the offspring and parent(s) are available to run simultaneously. This is required because subtle differences in experimental conditions can affect the results, and a DNA fingerprint run on the sire one week is not suitable for comparison to that of a putative offspring the next week.

GENETIC TESTING

New methods of identifying genetic markers are appearing at a rapid rate. A marker is simply a genetic sequence that is closely linked or associated with the gene of interest so that there is a 100 percent correlation between the presence of the marker and the presence of the gene of interest. The marker may or may not have any direct relation to the function of the gene in question.

Among the most promising of these techniques is the use of microsatellites and bulk segregant analysis. Both of these methods involve the use of the PCR (polymerase chain reaction). Simply put, with PCR a piece of DNA can be copied and amplified to provide a sufficient amount for analysis. Very specific primers can be made to initiate DNA amplification only at the gene of interest. Microsatellites are repetitive sequences that can be used as markers for specific genes or directly for parentage analysis. Bulk segregant analysis looks for differences in the DNA product between two or more groups of dogs (e.g., affected versus nonaffected in the case of cataracts) when the same primer is used. Initial analysis involves running the product on a gel to determine the relative sizes of the pieces of DNA that were produced in the PCR. The next step would be to clone and sequence the product in order to identify it. The different PCR product can be further analyzed to try to identify the gene responsible for the trait or at least to identify a genetic difference close enough to the specific gene that it can serve as a marker for the gene.

ETHICAL CONSIDERATIONS

As genetic testing becomes available, breeders will be faced with the decision as to whether or not to have their stock tested for specific genetic traits. This will be most applicable in the case of traits controlled by a single gene whose deleterious form is recessive to a dominant "normal" gene. These are the traits most likely to trouble breeders since there is no indication that a dog is a carrier of a recessive trait until it is bred to another carrier and produces an affected puppy. By that time numerous puppies may have been produced, each of which has at least a 50 percent chance of being a carrier. This is why it is so difficult to breed a recessive gene out of a population.

With the advent of DNA-based techniques, dogs will be able to be screened for a variety of genetic traits. This will be a powerful tool for breeders because, at least theoretically, deleterious recessive genes can be bred out of a population in one generation by not breeding any dog that tests positive for the presence of the gene. But there are many genes, good and bad, so by concentrating on eliminating one trait a breeder can inadvertently increase the incidence of other traits.

In addition, it may turn out that the frequency of a gene is so high in a given breed that if all the dogs who carried the gene were eliminated from the population breeders would be left with a very small population to start over with. Breeding the remaining dogs would undoubtedly reveal the presence of additional recessive genes. Selection for or against any single gene or trait without regard for other characteristics is likely to do more harm than good in the long run.

The solution to such a dilemma, if indeed a recessive gene is found to have a high frequency in the population, is to continue using carriers in breeding programs, but only if they are superior individuals in other respects. If a genetic test is available to determine which dogs are carriers before they are bred, then no mating of two carriers should ever be done. It is hard to justify the possibility of knowingly producing an affected puppy in order to produce (maybe) an outstanding show dog.

As an example, consider juvenile cataracts in Boston Terriers. This problem is due to a simple recessive gene as demonstrated by test breedings (Thibeault, personal communication). Carriers are apparently unaffected, so there is no indication that a dog has this gene until it is bred to another carrier and produces an affected puppy. Because there is only a 25 percent chance of a cataract puppy being produced in such a mating, several litters may have to be produced before there is an indication that the parents are carriers. If a genetic test was available, carriers could be distinguished from noncarriers, and carrier-to-carrier matings could be avoided. If it turns out that the frequency of the cataract gene is relatively high, this would allow the judicious use of carriers that are otherwise outstanding individuals in breeding programs. Eventually this gene could be eliminated from the breeding population by selecting dogs of excellent type that are also not carriers of the cataract gene. Because puppies could be tested very early for the presence of this gene, decisions as to which individuals to invest in as breeding and show stock could be more clearly made.

Once genetic tests are available for a variety of traits, the criteria for selection by the breeder will be expanded beyond visual assessment of the dog. Obviously, those genetic traits that have the most significant impact on the health and/or soundness of the dog should have priority over those that affect cosmetic factors.

REFERENCES

Colling, D.T. and R. Saison. 1980. Canine blood groups. 2. Description of a new allele in the Tr-blood group system. *Anim. Blood Grps. Biochem. Genet.* 11: 13–20.

Jeffries, A.J. and D.B. Morton. 1987. DNA fingerprints of dogs and cats. *Animal Genetics.* 18: 1–15.

Juneja, R.K., ICJ. Arnold, B. Gahne, J. Bouw. 1987. Parentage testing of dogs using variants of blood proteins: Description of five new plasma protein polymorphisms. *Animal Genetics.* 18: 297–310.

Thibeault, Sl. Hereditary Juvenile Cataracts in the Boston Terrier. Personal Communication.

Conclusion

Over the first one hundred years of the Boston Terrier, there were the early breeders who formed and developed the breed, then those who studied everything done before them and through careful selection of breeding stock refined and improved the quality of the Boston Terrier. Now, with an opthamolic test available to certify clear-eyed Boston Terriers and with genetic tests to be available soon for identifying cataract carriers and possibly identifying carriers of other genetic defects, the future of the Boston Terrier looks bright.

But these and any other new tests to come will be of no benefit if we do not use them. We must breed very carefully to ensure that the Boston Terriers of the future are sound quality specimens that conform to the Standard. Most important, sound, quality Boston Terriers with friendly dispositions will grace homes across the country.

Ch. Kokad's Kid Romance won the Boston Terrier Club of America Specialty in 1978 under Leonne Brown Kelley and handled by Marie Ferguson. Kid was bred by Rose Coulter of Oklahoma and owned by Charles H. Schmidt of Indiana.

Appendix:
Best of Breed Winners
of the Boston Terrier
Club of America
Specialty Show

1920—Ch. Aces of Aces, owned by Charles H. O'Connor

1921—Ch. Lady of Leonora, owned by Charles H. O'Connor

1922—Ch. Fairlawn Full O'Fun, owned by Fairlawn Kennels

1923—Ch. Colbert's Dolly, owned by Charles H. O'Connor

1924—Ch. Fairlawn Full O'Fun, owned by Fairlawn Kennels

1925—Ch. Million Dollar Kid, owned by Cristo Kennels

1926—Ch. Million Dollar Kid, owned by Baro Kennels

1927—Dowser's I'm Alone, owned by Mrs. E. J. Dowser

1928—Mosholu Bearcat, owned by Mrs. M. C. McGlone

1929—Ch. Hagerty's Surprise, owned by William Cornbill

1930—Ch. Hagerty's Surprise, owned by Droll & Rosenbloom

1931—Ch. Million Dollar Kid Boots, owned by Mrs. Jesse Thornton

1932—Ch. Ace of Aces Aviator, owned by Charles O'Connor

1933—Ch. Million Dollar Kid Boots, owned by Mrs. Jesse Thornton

1934—Ch. Million Dollar Kid Boots, owned by Mrs. Jesse Thornton

1935—Ch. Ace of Aces Rebel, owned by Charles O'Connor

1936—Int. Ch. Rockefeller's Ace, owned by W. E. Ely

1937—Int. Ch. Elyria Easter Parade, owned by C. M. Deems

1938—Int. Ch. Royal Kid Regards, owned by Mrs. E. P. Anders

1939—Ch. Griffings Little Femma, owned by Anna M. Griffing

1940—Int. Ch. Royal Kid Regards, owned by Mrs. E. P. Anders

1941—Ch. H.M.S. Kiddie Boots Son, owned by Mrs. Don Smith

1942—Ch. H.M.S. Kiddie Boots Son, owned by Mrs. Don Smith

1943—Ch. Yankee Sweet Perfection, owned by Harry J. Freeman

1944—Ch. H.M.S. Kiddie Boots Son, owned by Mrs. Don Smith

1945—Ch. Yankee Sweet Perfection, owned by Emily Shire

1946—Clasen's Best Regards, owned by Irene C. Clasen

1947—Ch. Yankee Sweet Perfection, owned by Emily Shire

1948—Ch. Morsel's Bonnie Mae, owned by Morton Rosuck

1948—Ch. Hayes' Chiquita, owned by Edward Hayes

1949—Ch. Royal Top Model, owned by Mrs. E. P. Anders

1950—Int. Ch. Clasen's Mel-O-Nee Maid, owned by Bert Allen

1951—Ch. Fritzi Regards of Pequa, owned by Joseph Glaser

1952—Ch. Fritzi Regards of Pequa, owned by Joseph Glaser

1953—Ch. Lou's Challenge, owned by Louis Rudginsky

1954—Ch. Dorsey's Custom Made, owned by Mr. & Mrs. J. E. Dorsey

1955—Ch. Emporer's Lady D.T.S., owned by Fred & Mary Lucas

1956—Int. Ch. Grant's Royal Command, owned by Mrs. Parker Grant

1957—Ch. Hillcrest Pride, owned by John & Helen Tierney

1958—Int. Ch. Grant's Royal Command, owned by Mrs. Parker Grant

1959—Ch. Dunn's Petite Stepper, owned by Mr. & Mrs. John Donahue

1960—Ch. Personality's Bold Ruler, owned by Mr. & Mrs. Leonard Hunt

1961—Ch. B-B's Kim of Fellow, owned by Mr. & Mrs. R. J. Schulte

1962—Ch. Montecalvo's Little Whiz, II, owned by Frank Montecalvo

1963—Ch. Montecalvo's Little Whiz, II, owned by Frank Montecalvo

1964—Caesar of Clover Farm, owned by Miriam R. Ellinger

1965—Katinka's Miss Chappie, II, owned by Roy S. Kibler

1966—Am. & Can. Ch. Chappie's Little Stardust, owned by K. Eileen Hite, M.D.

1967—Saints Miracle of Nez Pousse, owned by Helen Wright & Flora Hayes

1968—Ch. Clasen's Elegant Lady, owned by Mrs. Walter M. Jeffords, Jr. & Michael Wolf

1969—Ch. Star Q's Brass Buttons, owned by K. Eileen Hite, MD

1970—Ch. Star Q's Brass Buttons, owned by K. Eileen Hite, MD

1971—Ch. Star Q's Brass Buttons, owned by K. Eileen Hite, MD

1972—Ch. Beau Kay's Gay Chappie, owned by Mrs. Walter M. Jeffords, Jr. & Michael Wolf

1973—Ch. Tops Again Faust, owned by Alice Shea

1974—Ch. Karadin Our Mariah, owned by Ethel Braunstein, Ron Clark, and Col. Francisco Badrena

1975—Ch. O'Hooey's Lucky Boots, owned by Dorothy M. Hooey

1976—Ch. El-Hi's Star Q Colonel Butono, owned by Col. Francisco Badrena

1977—Nez Pousse's Me Too Festus, owned by Kathleen & John Kelly

1978—Ch. Kokad's Kid Romance, owned by Charles H. Schmidt

1979—Ch. Cydnee's Timothy Patrick, owned by Ruth M. Lieberg

1980–1984   No Shows

1985—Ch. Staley's El-Bo's Showman, owned by Michael & Beverly Staley

1986—Ch. Stone's Bo Dusty La Lorr's, owned by Patricia & Robert Stone

1987—Ch. Alexander's Cool Breeze, owned by Linda Alexander

1988—Ch. Maestro's Billy Whiz Bang, owned by Robert Breum & J. Martell

1989—Ch. El-Bo's Rudy is a Dandy, owned by Eleanor & Bob Candland

1990—Ch. Ri-Ja's Bronco Billy, owned by Richard & Mary Jane Craven

Ch. Alexander's Cool Breeze won the Boston Terrier Club of America Specialty under Warren Ubberoth in 1987. She is owned by Dr. and Mrs. Jim Alexander of Georgia.

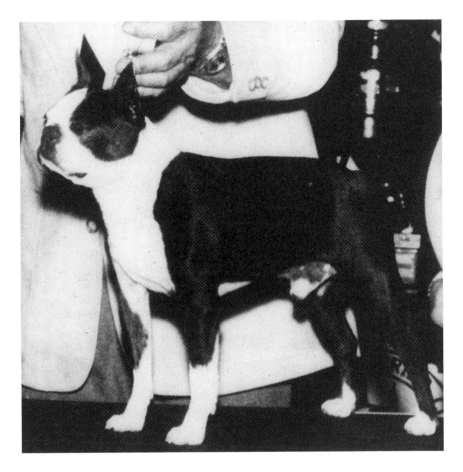

Ch. El-Bo's Rudy is a Dandy won the Boston Terrier Club of America Specialty from the Veterans class in 1989 under Maryann Caruso. Rudy was handled by breeder/owner Bob Candland.

Ch. Ri-Ja's Bronco Billy won the 1990 Boston Terrier Club of America Specialty. He was bred and owned by Richard and Jane Craven of Nebraska.

Ch. Barra's Highland Lassie won the 1992 Boston Terrier Club of America Specialty under Connie Hunter. She was owned by Elizabeth McNeil of Maryland and handled by Jodi Ghaster.

Ch. Al-Mar's By Invitation Only won the 1993 Boston Terrier Club of America Specialty. He was bred and owned by Patrice and Susan Kennedy of Arizona.

1991—Ch. Good News Daring Dakota, owned by Rhonda Watts

1992—Ch. Barra's Highland Lassie, owned by Elizabeth McNeil

1993—Ch. Al-Mar's By Invitation Only, owned by Patrice & Susan Kennedy

Glossary

A

AKC: American Kennel Club

Angulation: The angles formed by the bones at the joints, with the front angulation being formed by the shoulder and the upper arm, and the rear angulation being formed at the hock and stifle

Apple head: a rounded, dome-topped skull

Artificial insemination: Manual insertion of semen into the female's reproductive tract

B

Back: The topline of the dog from the withers to the croup

Balance: The relation by which all parts are in proportion to each other and are symmetrical

Bandy legs: Outward bend of legs

Barrel: Round rib region

Bat ear: An ear broad at the base and rounded at the top, which stands erect and faces forward; a natural ear

Bitch: A female dog

Bite: The relation of the upper and lower teeth when the mouth is closed (even, overshot, or undershot)

Blaze: The white marking running up the center of the face from the muzzle to the top of the skull and between the eyes

Blocky: Square

Brisket: The lower part of the chest in front of and between the forelegs

Brood Bitch: Female used for breeding

Brow: The ridge formed above the eye by the contour of the frontal bone

Butterfly nose: A partially unpigmented nose that appears to be speckled with flesh color

C

CD (Companion Dog): Obedience title awarded by the AKC to dogs who have attained the required scores in Novice classes at three Obedience Trials

CDX (Companion Dog Excellent): Obedience title awarded by the AKC to dogs who have attained the required scores in Open classes at three Obedience Trials

Champion (CH): Conformation title awarded by the AKC to dogs who have accumulated fifteen points (two of which must be majors wins of three or more points under different judges)

Cheeky: Thick, rounded cheeks that protrude on the sides of the skull

China eye: A clear, light blue, whitish, specked, or spotted blue eye

Chiseled: Clean-cut muzzle delicately cut away in front of eyes

Chops: Jowls or pendulous flesh of the lips and jaw

Close-coupled: Short from the last rib to the hindquarters

Coarse: Lacking refinement

Cobby: Compact, short body

Collar: White marking around the neck

Condition: Overall general health as exhibited by coat, muscle, general appearance, and carriage

Conformation: Total form and shape of all parts of the dog required by the breed standard

Congenital: Existing prior to or at birth

Coupling: The loins that lie between the ribs and the pelvis

Cow-hocked: Hocks that turn inward while turning rear feet out

Cropping: Surgical trimming of ears

Crossing over: Faulty gait resulting from twisting elbows, which results in crisscross movement and toeing out

Croup: Pelvic girdle including sacrum and surrounding area

Cryptorchid: Dog whose testicles are retained in the abdomen and have not normally descended into the scrotum. If the condition is bilateral, neither testicle has descended. If the condition is unilateral, one testicle is retained and the other has descended

Cushion: Fullness or thickness of the upper lip

D

Dam: Female parent

Dewclaw: A functionless toe on the inside of the foreleg

Dewlap: Loose-hanging skin under the throat and neck

Dish-faced: Slight concave profile when viewed from the side

Dock: Shortening of the tail, which is a disqualification

Dog: Male dog; or, collectively, both males and females

Domed: Evenly rounded skull; convex, not flat

Down-faced: Downward slope of muzzle from skull to tip of nose

Down in pasterns: Pasterns set at an incorrect angle causing bend in pasterns

Drive: Solid extending movement of the hindquarters

Dudley nose: Flesh-colored nose

E

East-West Front: Incorrect front in which the feet turn out, facing away from each other

Elbows out: Elbows that turn out from the body and are not held straight and close to the body

Even bite: Meeting of upper and lower incisors with a level bite and no overlap

Expression: Combination of all features of head and face, including size, shape, and placement of ears and eyes, to produce a special look of softness and intelligence

F

Fiddle front: Forelegs out at elbows with pasterns close and feet turned out

Flank: The side of the body between the last rib and the hip

Flews: Hanging part of the upper lips

Forequarters: The front assembly from the shoulders down to the feet

Foster mother: A bitch used to nurse puppies that are not hers

Frogface: Receding under jaw with an overshot upper jaw

Front: The forequarters as viewed head on

Furrow: Slight indentation down the center of the skull to the stop

G

Gait: The pattern of movement distinguished by particular rhythm and footfall

Gay tail: A tail carried above the horizontal

Gestation: The sixty-three-day period of embryo development from fertilization to whelping

H

Hackney gait: The high lifting of the front feet like that of a Hackney horse

Hare foot: A long narrow foot in which the two center toes are longer than the end toes; this gives the appearance of a rabbit's foot

Haw: A third eyelid on the inside corner of the eye

Heat: Seasonal period of the female lasting approximately twenty-one days and occurring approximately every six months

Hindquarters: Rear assembly of the dog

Hock: The collection of bones of the hind leg forming the lower joint between the thigh and the metatarsus

I

Inbreeding: The breeding of very closely related dogs of the same breed; for example, mother/son, father/daughter, brother/sister

L

Layback: The angle of the shoulder blade as compared with the vertical plane viewed from the side

Linebreeding: The mating of dogs of the same breed within the line or family to one or more common ancestors in the first few generations

Lippy: Loose hanging lips

Loaded shoulders: Excessive development of the muscles of the shoulder blades

Loin: Lumbar region from the ribs to the pelvic girdle

M

Monorchid: A dog having only one testicle in the scrotum

Muzzle: The head in front of the eyes; nasal bone, nostrils, and jaws

Muzzle band: White marking around the muzzle

N

Neck well set-on: Good neckline that blends smoothly with the withers to flow into the topline

Nick: A breeding that produces quality puppies

O

Out at elbows: Elbows that turn out from the body instead of being held close

Out at shoulders: Shoulder blades that are loosely attached to the body and cause the shoulders to jut out and increase the width of the front

Outcrossing: The mating of unrelated dogs of the same breed

Overshot: The incisors of the upper jaw project beyond the incisors of the lower jaw, causing a space between the upper and lower incisors

P

Paddling: A gaiting fault named for its resemblance to the movement of canoe paddles. The front legs swing forward in a stiff arc

Pastern: The region of the foot between the pastern joint and the foot

Pedigree: A written record of a dog's ancestors for three generations or more

R

Rangy: Tall, long in body, high on leg, often lightly framed

Roach back: An arched spine with the curvature rising behind the withers and carried over the loins

Rolling gate: Swaying, ambling action of the rear when moving

Screw tail: A naturally short tail twisted in more or less spiral formation

Sire: The male parent

Slab sided: Flat sides with insufficient spring of ribs

Sloping shoulders: The shoulder blade laid back

Smooth coat: Short hair, close lying

Snipey: A muzzle that is too pointed, weak, or narrow and that lacks depth and breadth

Soundness: The condition of health by which all parts and organs are functioning normally and are in relation to each other

Spay: The surgical removal of the bitch's ovaries to prevent conception

Splash-marked: Irregular patch of white on color

Splayfoot: A flat foot with toes spread

Spring of ribs: Curvature of ribs to allow for heart and lung capacity

Square body: One whose measurements from the withers to the ground equals the measurements from the forechest to the rump

Standard: The description of the ideal dog of each breed, which serves as a word pattern by which dogs are judged

Station: Comparative height from the ground, such as medium stationed

Stifle: The joint above the hock in the hind leg that corresponds to the knee in humans

Stop: The step up from the muzzle to the back of the skull, the indentation between the eyes where the nasal bones and cranium meet

Substance: Strength of bone

Swayback: Sagging, concave curvature of the spine from the withers to the hip bone

T

Tail set: The way the base of the tail sets on the rump

Ticking: Small isolated areas of black hairs that spot the white

Topline: The line from just behind the withers to the tail set

Tuck-up: Small waisted, shallower body depth at the loin

Type: The distinguishing characteristics of a breed that embody the Standard's essentials

U

UD (Utility Dog): AKC Obedience title awarded to dogs who have attained the required scores in Utility classes at three Obedience Trials

Undershot: The front teeth (incisors) of the lower jaw project beyond the front teeth of the upper jaw when the mouth is closed

Unsound: A dog incapable of functioning normally

W

Walleye: An eye with a blue or whitish iris

Well let-down: Short hocks

Withers: The region between the shoulder bones at their highest point

Wrinkle: Loose-folding skin on forehead and foreface

Wry mouth: Improper alignment of upper and lower jaws; cross bite, twisted

The Authors

Beverly and Michael Staley were both born into homes with Boston Terriers. They had a pet Boston Terrier, Lady, when they were first married, but they did not begin exhibiting and breeding Boston Terriers until 1975. Since that time they have bred numerous champions. Michael has owner-handled many to their championships and Specials careers, and one, Ch. Staley's El-Bo's Showman, became a multiple Best in Show winner. Michael Staley has judged Boston Terriers since 1991. Both Staleys have held various offices in the Boston Terrier Club of Greater Cincinnati, and Beverly Staley is a past secretary of the Boston Terrier Club of America.